OUT OF
CONTROL

Also by Zbigniew Brzezinski

The Soviet Bloc: Unity and Conflict (1960)
Between Two Ages: America's Role in the Technetronic Era (1970)
Power and Principle: Memoirs of the National Security Adviser, 1977–1981 (1983)
Game Plan: A Geostrategic Framework for the Conduct of the U.S.–Soviet Contest (1986)
The Grand Failure: The Birth and Death of Communism in the Twentieth Century (1989)

OUT OF CONTROL

Global Turmoil on the Eve of the
Twenty-First Century

Zbigniew Brzezinski

Collier Books
Macmillan Publishing Company
New York

Maxwell Macmillan Canada
Toronto

Maxwell Macmillan International
New York   Oxford   Singapore   Sydney

Collier Books   Maxwell Macmillan Canada, Inc.
Macmillan Publishing Company   1200 Eglinton Avenue East
866 Third Avenue   Suite 200
New York, NY 10022   Don Mills, Ontario M3C 3N1

Macmillan Publishing Company is part of the Maxwell Communication Group of Companies.

Library of Congress Cataloging-in-Publication Data
Brzezinski, Zbigniew K., 1928–
Out of control: global turmoil on the eve of the twenty-first
century / Zbigniew Brzezinski.—1st Collier Books ed.
p.   cm.
Includes index.
ISBN 0-02-008115-4
1. World politics—1989–   2. Communism—History—20th century.
3. Post-communism.   4. United States—Foreign relations—1993–
I. Title.
D860.B79   1994
909.82'9—dc20
93–35653   CIP

First Collier Books Edition 1994

10   9   8   7   6   5   4   3   2

Printed in the United States of America

Contents

Introduction   ix

Part I   The Politics of Organized Insanity   1

   1   The Century of Megadeath   7
   2   The Centrality of Metamyth   19
   3   Coercive Utopia   32

Part II   Beyond Political Awakening   45

   1   The Victory of Small Beliefs   57
   2   Permissive Cornucopia   64
   3   Philosophical Polarization   75

Part III   The Peerless Global Power   85

   1   The Paradox of Global Power   91
   2   The Dissonant Message   102
   3   The Faceless Rivals   116

Part IV   Dilemmas of Global Disorder   147

   1   The Geopolitical Vacuum   155
   2   The Vengeful Phoenix   167
   3   The Giant of Global Inequality   182

Part V   The Illusion of Control   201

  Acknowledgments   233
  Index   235

To Jimmy Carter
whose message of human rights
continues to resonate

Introduction

This book is not a prediction but an urgent warning. It is about the state of global politics today, about what may happen by the onset of the twenty-first century, and also about *what must not be allowed to happen.* My concern that global change is out of control involves a necessarily subjective interpretation of the political meaning and message of our times. It is hence partially diagnosis, partially prognosis, and partially advocacy.

This personal statement occasionally even trespasses on the philosophical. But it is not possible to deal with modern global politics, in the age of massive political awakening, without taking into account the consequences not only of enhanced human capabilities but also of changes in the dominant content of the human spirit.

Recognition of the notable acceleration in the velocity of our history and the uncertainty of its trajectory is the necessary point of departure for my argument. History has not ended but has become compressed. Whereas in the past, historical epochs stood out in relatively sharp relief, and one could thus have a defined sense of historical progression, history today entails sharp discontinuities that collide with each other, condense our sense of perspective, and confuse our historical perceptions.

In other words, we live in a world that is already in fact very different from the one which we have begun to comprehend, and by the time our comprehension has caught up with the new reality, the world is likely to be even more drastically different in ways that today may seem unthinkable. Discontinuity is the central reality of our contemporary history, and that demands an intensified debate regarding the meaning of our era.

Moreover, our ability to understand the wider ramifications of the present—not to speak of the future—is impeded by the massive collapse, especially in the advanced parts of the world, of almost all established *values*. Totalitarian doctrines have been discredited—and that is to be applauded. But the role of religion in defining moral standards has also declined while an ethos of consumerism masquerades as a substitute for *ethical standards*. Humanity's capacity to control itself and its environment has been expanding exponentially and our material expectations even more so. At the same time, our societal criteria of moral discernment and of self-control have become increasingly vague. Ethical perplexity does not enhance historical comprehension.

This book is based on a central premise: that ultimately it is ideas that mobilize political action and thus shape the world. Such ideas may be simple or complex, good or bad, well understood or just instinctively felt. At times they may be articulated by charismatic personalities; at other times, they may be just pervasively present. Ours is the age of global political awakening, and hence political ideas are likely to be increasingly central, either as the source of intellectual cohesion or of confusion, as well as of political consensus or of conflict.

I focus more specifically on three broad questions:

1. What is the historical significance of the grand failure during the twentieth century of totalitarianism in general and of communism in particular as an ideological force in world affairs?

2. What is the likely doctrinal and geopolitical shape of the world as it enters the twenty-first century?

3. What are the implications of the foregoing for America's role in the world and also for American society itself?

These are large questions. They are also complex, timely, and important. I try to address them not in an extended, heavily documented, and rather academic volume—but through a direct personal statement. I want to leave the reader with a clear grasp of my argument, so that he or she can then decide whether my case is compelling or dubious. I should make it clear, however, that *this is not a policy book*, with a list of instant solutions for complex problems. The issues that I discuss are intractable, deeply rooted in long-term historical tides, and their correction requires first a profound reassessment of basic political and social values.

That case is derived in part from some of my previous books. In *Between Two Ages* (1970) I argued that America was plunging into a new era ahead of most of the world, and that this explained both America's troubles and its promise, while the Soviet Union was likely to remain mired in the early stages of its industrial development. I return to some of these themes in this book. In *Game Plan* (1986) I made the case that the United States could prevail peacefully in the Cold War, especially given the internal weaknesses of the Soviet system. *The Grand Failure: The Birth and Death of Communism in the Twentieth Century* (1989), as the title suggests, postulated that communism had spent its force and that the world was now entering the postcommunist phase of history.

The argument developed in what follows unfolds through four stages:

1. Twentieth-century politics, dominated by the rise of totalitarian movements, deserve to be described as the politics of organized insanity. That insanity produced not only unparalleled bloodshed but involved also the most ambitious attempt in mankind's history to establish total control over both the internal and the external condition of the human being itself. The failed attempt to create coercive utopias—that is, heavens on earth—on the basis of dogmatic designs of truly cosmic brazenness perverted the rational and the idealistic impulses unleashed in Europe some two hundred years ago by the French Revolution.

2. The failure of the totalitarian experiments coincided with the political awakening of mankind on a truly global scale. This coincidence may mean that the liberal democratic framework, now associated with both the French and American revolutions, is potentially applicable on a worldwide basis, thereby creating the basis for a possible worldwide political consensus. However, disintegrative forces globally at work could still prove more potent than integrative forces. *The global relevance of the West's political message could be vitiated by the growing tendency in the advanced world to infuse the inner content of liberal democracy with a life-style that I define as permissive cornucopia. The priority given to individual self-gratification, combined with the growing capacity of the human being to reshape itself through genetic and other forms of scientific self-alteration—with neither subject to moral restraint—tend to create a condition in which little self-control is exercised over the dynamics of the desire to consume and to tinker with the self.* In contrast, outside the richer West, much of human life is still dominated by fundamental concerns with survival and not with conspicuous consumption. These divergent trends undermine

and inhibit global consensus and enhance the dangers inherent in a deepening global cleavage.

3. Today, the United States stands as the only truly global power. But it does so in a setting in which traditional international politics are being transformed into global politics: politics that are becoming—under the influence of modern communications and increasing economic interpenetration—an extended process, obliterating the distinction between the domestic and the international. Inherent in this is the potential for the emergence of a genuine global community. *The question arises whether a global power that is not guided by a globally relevant set of values can for long exercise that predominance.* To be sure, American power is real, and in fact, it is unlikely to be challenged in the foreseeable future by any of its potential rivals. Neither Japan nor Europe—for reasons stated in this section—are in fact likely to displace America. In that sense, the U.S. global position is historically unique. But many of the weaknesses of a permissive cornucopia represent the potentially defining trend in the current American culture. *Unless there is some deliberate effort to reestablish the centrality of some moral criteria for the exercise of self-control over gratification as an end in itself, the phase of American preponderance may not last long, despite the absence of any self-evident replacement.*

4. Although a single and increasingly interdependent global political process is emerging, America's difficulty in exercising effective global authority within it—because of inner weaknesses derived more from cultural than from economic causes—could produce a situation of intensifying global instability. On the geopolitical level, that is likely to be expressed through the intensification of Eurasian regional conflicts which are ensuing in the wake of the Soviet Union's collapse. Proliferation of weapons of mass destruction makes this prospect more ominous. The crisis in the postcommunist world in the meantime could deepen, undermining the wider global appeal of democracy and stimulat-

ing the reappearance of millennial demagogy. The conflicts between the North and the South could also then sharpen. A new coalition of the poorer nations against the rich—perhaps led by China—might then emerge.

The interaction between the acceleration of our history, our increased capacities to shape the world, our rapidly expanding material desires, and our moral ambiguity is thus generating unprecedented dynamics of uncontrolled change. We are all racing into the future but it is increasingly the pace of change, and not our wills, which is shaping that future. The world is rather like a plane on automatic pilot, with its speed continuously accelerating but with no defined destination.

To be sure, there are some hopeful signs that in the wake of the Cold War's end mankind may now be in a better position to undertake a more serious effort to organize itself as a global community. That notwithstanding, the central fact remains that humanity's ability to define for itself a meaningful existence is increasingly threatened by the contradiction between subjective expectations and objective socioeconomic conditions. Inherent in the potential collision between these two broad trends is the danger that world politics—both in terms of international affairs and of internal societal conditions—could simply spiral out of control, generating massive political disorder and philosophical confusion.

This is why there is the need for a wider, globally shared understanding of the purpose of political existence—that is, the condition of human interdependence. A major step toward such understanding implies some effort at defining the proper limits—ultimately, *moral in character*—of internal and external aspirations. This will require a conscious effort to strike a balance between social need and personal gratification, global poverty and national wealth, irresponsible alteration of the physical environment as well as even of the human being and the effort to preserve both nature's patrimony and the authenticity of human identity.

This is the critical historical challenge that America now faces in the postutopian age. The point of departure for an effective response is the recognition that only by creating a society that is guided by some shared criteria of self-restraint can it help to shape a world more truly in control of its destiny. Only with such recognition can we ensure that we will be the masters, and not the victims, of history as we enter the twenty-first century.

Zbigniew Brzezinski
Northeast Harbor, Maine
AUGUST 1992

PART I

The Politics of Organized Insanity

The twentieth century was born in hope. It dawned in a relatively benign setting. The principal powers of the world had enjoyed, broadly speaking, a relatively prolonged spell of peace. Only three major eruptions of international violence had disrupted the basic tranquility sustained by the system established during the Congress of Vienna of 1815. The Crimean War of 1853–56 briefly pitted France and Britain against Russia, but without major geopolitical repercussions; while the Franco-Prussian War of 1870–71 and the Russo-Japanese War of 1904–1905 signaled the emergence on the world scene of Germany and of Japan, respectively, as new potential major actors.

The dominant mood in the major capitals as of January 1, 1900 was generally one of optimism. The structure of global power seemed stable. Existing empires appeared to be increasingly enlightened as well as secure. Some, like the Austro-Hungarian, could even have been said to be examples of both moderation and ethnic cohabitation. The principal capitals, be they London or Paris or Berlin or Vienna or St. Petersburg, were beginning to enjoy the benefits of the industrial revolution

3

while thriving also as cultural centers. Art, architecture, literature were blooming, with innovative currents generating a mood
of hopeful creativity. Democracy, and even social democracy,
was also beginning to make modest inroads into the existing
traditional authoritarian structures, but without visibly disruptive
effects. Social inequality, though widespread, seemed still normal but increasingly subject—at least in such places as, for
example, Germany—to gradual correction by progressively expanding governmental intervention.

Most importantly, the dominant political outlook, at least on
the surface, seemed to be relatively passionless. Nationalism was
becoming stronger, but it was not yet dominant. The ruling elites
partook of the considerable degree of consensus, not to speak
of blood ties, that prevailed among their reigning monarchs.
Growing faith in the scientific revolution was generating optimism about the future condition of mankind. The onset of the
twentieth century was hailed in many commentaries as the real
beginning of the Age of Reason.

And reason expressed through science, indeed, did help to
transform the world for the better. The twentieth century experienced unprecedented scientific breakthroughs in the areas most
directly relevant to the physical aspects of the human condition:
medicine, nutrition, modern communications. The scourge of
epidemics, of child mortality, of vulnerability to various diseases
was dramatically reduced. Human life expectancy increased by
30 to 50 percent in many parts of the world. Innovations in
surgery and in general medical treatment as well as the breakout
into outer space dramatically redefined the frontiers of human
life. *But this progress, unfortunately, was not matched on the moral
level—with politics representing the twentieth century's greatest
failure.*

Contrary to its promise, the twentieth century became
mankind's most bloody and hateful century, a century of halluci-

natory politics and of monstrous killings. Cruelty was institutionalized to an unprecedented degree, lethality was organized on
a mass production basis. The contrast between the scientific
potential for good and the political evil that was actually unleashed is shocking. Never before in history was killing so globally pervasive, never before did it consume so many lives, never
before was human annihilation pursued with such concentration
of sustained effort on behalf of such arrogantly irrational goals.

Admittedly, there have been other periods in history in which
violence was intense. With the population of the world during
the Middle Ages so much smaller, the Great Horde's sweep
through central Europe, and also into the Middle East, produced, on a relative scale, perhaps even higher mortality. Nonetheless, this as well as other comparable explosions of violence
were essentially outbursts—intense, violent, bloody but rarely
sustained. Slaughter, especially of noncombatants, was directly
associated with physical contest and conquest; rarely was it a
matter of sustained policy, based on systematized premeditation.
It is the latter that represents the twentieth century's gruesome
contribution to political history.

ONE

The Century of Megadeath

It is not necessary to chronicle in detail this century's bloody record of mass murder on a scale beyond human capacity to fully comprehend and to truly empathize. But a concise statistical accounting of the extraordinary toll of politically motivated killings is a necessary point of departure for defining this century's political meaning and legacy. (The enormity of that toll deserves to be described in terms of *megadeaths*, mega being a factor of 10^6.)

The unprecedented dimensions of the twentieth century's bloodletting were directly derived from the central existential struggles that defined and dominated this century. These struggles cumulatively produced the two most massive moral outrages of our time—outrages that transformed the century of promise into one of organized insanity. The first involved prolonged and extraordinarily devastating wars, not only with very high military casualties but with an equally high or even higher civilian toll: two world wars and at least thirty additional major international or civil wars (defined as ones in which fatalities were no less than tens of thousands). The second has involved the totalitarian

attempts to create what might be described as "coercive utopias": perfect societies based on the physical elimination of pre-
scribed "social misfits," doctrinally defined as racially or socially
precluded from redemption.

Precise figures on the cumulative toll are not possible. Some
of the combatant states—especially the victorious ones—kept
reasonably accurate statistics for their own casualties; the van-
quished often suffered the loss of their archives and hence only
estimates are possible. The problem of accounting is even more
acute in regard to civilian deaths that occurred as by-products
of the war. Even in the case of advanced countries, such as
Germany or Japan, the loss of life caused by air attacks can only
be estimated. The problem is especially acute in the case of
civilian deaths in countries like the Soviet Union or China,
where combat also entailed foreign occupation, massive social
disruptions, and the collapse of organized governmental institutions.

More elusive still are the totals of the deaths inflicted by
totalitarian regimes in pursuit of ther doctrinal agendas of hatred.
Neither Hitler nor Stalin nor Mao boasted publicly of their
programs of mass murder. But the deliberate killings of the Jews,
or of the Gypsies, or of the Poles cannot be counted as civilian
by-products of the war. Conquest through war made their killing
possible, but they were killed deliberately and not concurrently
with military operations. This was also the case with the massive
internal social annihilations carried out by Lenin, Stalin, and
Mao.

The figures that follow are, therefore, estimates; but what is
important is the *scale* and not the exact numbers. It is the scale—
so unprecedented that it becomes almost incomprehensible—
that provides a gruesome measure both for the political passions
of the century and for the technological means that the passions
were able to harness. (In rounding out the totals, middle esti-

mates were accepted—hence the totals that follow are, if anything, perhaps somewhat low.)

Of those killed in twentieth-century wars, approximately 33,000,000 were young men, mostly between the ages of eighteen and thirty, who perished in the name of nationalism and/or ideology. The two world wars are counted to have consumed at least 8,500,000 and 19,000,000 military lives, respectively, causing a massive biological depletion of talent, energy, and genetic inheritance in several key European nations. Other wars elsewhere in this century caused an additional 6,000,000 or so military fatalities. Civilian casualties—as actual by-product of hostilities (and not of deliberate genocide)—accounted for about 13,000,000 women, children, and older men during World War I and for about 20,000,000 during World War II, to which must be added the estimated 15,000,000 civilian Chinese deaths in the Sino-Japanese war which started prior to World War II.

In addition, probably no less than 6,000,000 civilians perished in other conflicts. Among them, the Mexican wars of the early century, the Paraguay-Bolivia War of 1928–35, the Spanish Civil War of 1936–39, the Italian invasion of Ethiopia in 1936, the India-Pakistan partition of 1947 and the subsequent two wars, the Korean war of 1950–53, the Nigerian civil war of 1967, the Vietnam War of 1961–75, and the Iraq-Iran war of 1980–87 have been the most lethal.

In the process, killing became devastatingly indiscriminate, with civilians perishing in numbers at least as great as the military fatalities. Moreover, even worse from the moral point of view was the pervasive inclination of all combatants to view enemy civilians as legitimate targets. Although it was the Nazis and the Japanese militarists who initiated the practice of total war, democratic societies—once also at war—likewise succumbed to the tempting proposition that "the ends justify the means." The hundreds of thousands of innocent civilians killed in the firebombing of Dresden and in the atomic destruction of Hiroshima provide mute testimony to the moral corruption facilitated by advances in the technology of death.

In brief, this century's wars extinguished no less than approximately *87,000,000 lives*, with the numbers of wounded, maimed, or otherwise afflicted being beyond estimate.

These staggering numbers are matched and morally even overshadowed by a still more horrifying total, one that justifiably stamps the twentieth century as the century of megadeath: the number of defenseless individuals deliberately put to death because of doctrinal hatred and passions. Four individuals—each epitomizing a doctrine in which the physical elimination not just of individual opponents but of entire categories of human beings, defined either through race or class, was held to be socially beneficial—caused most of these politically motivated deaths.

In the name of doctrine, Hitler caused the deliberate killing of over 5,000,000 Jews (since the round figure of 6,000,000 is usually cited, it should be noted that precise tables with supporting data, providing a detailed breakdown of the Nazi genocide of the Jews, are contained in the monumental study by Raul Hilberg, *The Destruction of the European Jews* [1985], with the horrendous toll amounting to no less than 5,100,000); about 800,000 Gypsies—with both Jews and Gypsies designated for total extinction; more than 2,000,000 Poles, with special efforts made to kill the entire Polish intelligentsia; perhaps as many as 6,000,000 Soviet (mostly Russian and Ukrainian) prisoners of war and civilians murdered or starved to death deliberately (beyond the millions killed in combat or as a consequence of combat and already included in the war totals); and at least 2–3,000,000 cold-bloodedly murdered elsewhere in Europe, with Yugoslavia alone accounting for about one-half of the victims. The Jewish holocaust included about 2,000,000 children deliberately murdered, by far the most gruesome case of infanticide in human history. In brief, Hitler had about 17,000,000 human beings put to death.

He was outdone, however, by Stalin and Mao. Stalin inherited from Lenin an efficiently operating machinery for the mass destruction of political and social opponents, and he further improved on it. Because of Lenin—through mass executions during and after civil war, through massive deaths in the Gulag initiated under Lenin's direction (and powerfully documented in Solzhenitsyn's *Gulag Archipelago*), and through mass famines induced by ruthless indifference (with Lenin callously dismissing as unimportant the deaths of "the half-savage, stupid, difficult people of the Russian villages")—it can be estimated that between 6–8,000,000 people perished.

That number subsequently was more or less tripled by Stalin, who caused, it has been conservatively estimated, the deaths of no less than 20,000,000 people, and perhaps even upward of 25,000,000. Of that total, in the years 1937–38 alone, 1,000,000 were shot one by one and an additional 2,000,000 died in labor camps. An additional 1,000,000 were also executed during the preceding years, following Stalin's accession to power in the late 1920s. Several million died during the collectivization and the artificially induced great famine of the early 1920s. Robert Conquest (in his pioneering and monumental *The Great Terror*) estimates that, all in all, approximately 7,000,000 were the victims of Stalin's destruction of the peasant society and that about 12,000,000 died in labor camps. To this must be added another 1,000,000 or so put to death during and after World War II; the victims of ruthless mass deportations prior to, during, and after World War II; and the mass killings and deportations of Poles in occupied Poland and of Balts between 1939 and 1941 and again during the waning phases and in the aftermath of World War II.

In addition, Stalinist Russia had a gruesome record in its treatment of prisoners of war. According to data compiled in 1992 by the Germans, some 357,000 German POWs died in Soviet captivity during and after the war. In addition, several hundred thousand Japanese, Rumanian, Hungarian, Finnish, and Italian POWs also perished without a trace in Soviet camps. Finally, of the 180,000 Polish military captured by the Soviets in 1939, only about 40,000 subsequently reappeared. Thus close to 1,000,000 POWs can be assumed to have died in Stalin's camps.

To this day, the former Soviet Union is dotted with enormous secret graveyards, usually located on the outskirts of big cities— often in parks reserved for NKVD dachas and sometimes in abandoned mine shafts—in which the bodies of the executed victims were systematically (usually at night) buried. Just next to Minsk (a city of less than 1 million inhabitants in Stalin's time), a burial site containing some 200,000 executed victims was uncovered in the late 1980s. Subsequently, similar sites have been found throughout the entire land, next to every major city.

Most of those killed were executed in the most perfunctory, almost impersonal manner. To the Bolshevik leaders, the process involved was one of class cleansing, in which the society was purified by the "liquidation" of entire categories of enemies. Documents unearthed from the Soviet archives (following the collapse of the Soviet Union) reveal an attitude toward killing on the part of the Soviet leaders which was pathologically deprived of any humane feelings, not to speak of the fundamental contravention of any civilized notions of judicial procedures. Killing simply became a bureaucratic function, both for the leaders commanding it and for the executioners performing it.

In that respect, the mass murder of the Jews by the Nazis or of class enemies by the Communists had much in common, in both cases becoming a totally dehumanized process, devoid even of passion, not to speak of compassion.

A chilling case in point is provided by the documents which Boris Yeltsin courageously revealed to the world regarding the long-kept secret Soviet massacre in 1940 of Polish officers, officials, and intellectuals taken prisoner after the joint Nazi-Soviet occupation of Poland in 1939. On March 5, 1940, L. Beria, the head of the NKVD, submitted a memorandum addressed "To Comrade Stalin," providing a detailed breakdown of the 14,736 officers held prisoner in three camps, and of 10,685 Polish political prisoners held in various Soviet prisons. All were described as committed enemies of the Soviet Union, and the document recommended that they all be executed. On the same day, the Politburo met, and its protocol no. 13 of March 5, 1940 simply stated as follows:

> Decision of 5.III.1940—Case of NKVD USSR
> I. To Convey to the NKVD USSR
> 1) the files of 14,700 persons contained in camps for prisoners of war: former Polish officers, officials, landowners, policemen, intelligence officials, gendarmes, settlers and criminals,
> 2) as well as the files of 11,000 persons arrested and placed in prisons in the western regions of Ukraine and Belorussia: members of various counterrevolutionary, espionage and diversionary organizations, former landowners, factory owners, former Polish officers, officials and refugees—to resolve through a special process, applying to them the highest penalty: shooting.
> II. The cases are to be resolved without summoning the arrested and without presenting to them the indictments, the decisions to close the investigations and the verdict according to the following procedure:

a) regarding the persons held in camps for prisoners of war on the basis of data presented by the Administration for Prisoners of War of the NKVD USSR,

b) regarding persons arrested on the basis of data presented by the NKVD of the Ukrainian SSR and the NKVD of the Belorussian SSR.

III. Resolution of the cases and the handing down of the verdict is to be entrusted to the troika of comrades composed of: Merkulov, Kabulov and Bashtakov (head of the first Special Department of the NKVD USSR).

(signed) Secretary of the C.C. J. STALIN.

That was all. With one scrap of paper, containing the brief phrase "applying to them the highest penalty: shooting," more than 25,000 lives (representing in this particular case the social elite of a country) were wiped out. On a much more massive scale, this procedure was repeated for several years for hundreds of thousands of Soviet citizens, not to mention the millions that also perished through exhaustion, starvation, and maltreatment in the Gulag. Though the precise figures for Stalin's toll will never be available, it is unlikely that the range of 20–25,000,000 victims is an exaggeration. Census statistics also indicate that additionally the biological depletion of the Soviet population during Stalin's reign was even higher. The estimated number of killings cited above, in any case, accounts for Stalin's direct genocide. Demographic depletion—because of reduced birthrates, loss of offspring because of higher infant mortality, births that did not take place because of imprisonment of a would-be parent, etc.—certainly had to be in excess of even the enormous toll directly attributable to Stalin personally.

Stalin's methods were applied after 1945 throughout Eastern Europe. In every satellite state, concentration camps—in effect, death camps—were established, in which enemies of the new

regimes were worked to death. Tens of thousands thereby perished. The scale of individual executions throughout the con-
quered region cannot even be estimated, but it certainly
amounted to several hundred thousand. In some areas, where
active resistance to the imposition of communism was strongest—such as Poland, western Ukraine, Lithuania, and parts of
Yugoslavia—the killings were on a mass scale, often followed by
large-scale deportation of the local populace, suspected of aiding
the resistance. Once the Soviet Army drove the Germans out of
Poland, the Soviet NKVD and its Communist puppets were
especially ruthless in stamping out the anti-Nazi Polish underground, since it represented during World War II the best organized European resistance movement and was thus a formidable
barrier to Communist rule.

It is a moral outrage that in the wake of the extensive denunciation of Stalin's crimes throughout what was once called the
Soviet bloc, not a single Stalinist secret police functionary, concentration camp commander, torturer, or executioner has been
placed on trial for Stalinist crimes. To this day, former Nazi
war criminals are still being punished for their crimes against
humanity. The postcommunist Russian and East European press
has been filled with detailed accounts of massive mistreatment,
secret executions, gruesome tortures under interrogation, and
of the discovery after discovery of new mass graves of tens of
thousands of secretly buried victims. As the past is unmasked,
even memoirs of some former executioners have appeared in
print, in one Russian case with a former NKVD executioner
describing how he had improved the technique of shooting victims in the death cell without causing blood to be sprayed by
forcing the gun barrel into the mouths of the condemned. In
another notorious case, some of the executioners of the 15,000
Polish officers in Katyn and elsewhere have been identified as
living in the former Soviet Union on state pensions. Yet in a

strange display of moral lethargy, to this day nowhere has anyone been brought to justice for these extraordinary crimes.

Accounting for the human losses in China during the most violent phases of the communist experiment is an even more difficult task. Unlike the exposure of Stalin's crimes in the Soviet Union (and the much delayed and the still somewhat reticent exposure of Lenin's crimes), the Chinese regime persists in regarding the Maoist phase as relatively sacrosanct, with its killings justified but with their scale kept secret. The only exception is the cultural revolution of the late 1960s and early 1970s, from which the current Chinese rulers suffered directly. For this phase of internal violence some estimates have surfaced, and they suggest deaths on the scale of 1–2,000,000.

For the earlier phases, notably the 1950s, there have been broad estimates of as many as several million executed as "enemies of the people"—mostly landlords and richer bourgeoisie as well as former Kuomintang officials and officers. In addition, the figure of up to 27,000,000 peasants who perished as a consequence of the forcible collectivization has often been cited. Given the size of the Chinese population, and the indifference to human life of the current regime, the estimate of about 29,000,000 as the human cost of the communist era is in all probability on the low side, especially as it does not take into account the net loss to China's population because of the demographic impact of such mass killings.

This ghastly ledger would not be complete without some accounting of the price in human lives paid for the attempts to construct communist utopias in Eastern Europe, North Korea, Vietnam, Cambodia, and Cuba. It is a safe estimate that these consumed at least 3,000,000 victims, with Cambodia under Pol Pot alone accounting for about one-third. Thus the total might actually be higher. In brief, the failed effort to build communism in the twentieth century consumed the lives of almost 60,000,000 human beings, making communism the most costly human failure in all of history.

The above summary registers the human toll of the massive moral failures of the twentieth century. And that does not include even all of the most egregious cases. The massacre of the Armenians in Turkey during World War I or the Hindu-Moslem killings during the partition of India represent also historical stains of very major proportions, with religious and ethnic passions out of control prompting the deaths in all probability of no less than 3–4,000,000 people.

To sum up, the appalling total killed deliberately during this century—not in actual combat but in cold blood, for various ideological or religious reasons—comes to upward of *80,000,000 lives*.

Thus, during the twentieth century, no less than 167,000,000 lives—and quite probably in excess of 175,000,000—were deliberately extinguished through politically motivated carnage. That is the approximate equivalent of the total population of France, Italy, and Great Britain; or over two-thirds of the total current population of the United States. This is more than the total killed in *all* previous wars, civil conflicts, and religious persecutions throughout human history. These horrendous though dry numbers are also a reminder of what can happen when humanity's innate capacity for aggression becomes harnessed by dogmatic self-righteousness and is enhanced by increasingly potent technologies of destruction.

The above estimates of total deaths cannot convey—and, given their scale, the human mind cannot even comprehend— the cumulative damage and the moral degradation inherent in the twin cataclysms of the twentieth century: its massive wars and its totalitarian revolutions. Europe, the cradle of Western civilization, was subjected (in the course of two world wars) to more than ten years of sustained destruction and massive killings. China and Japan suffered similar fates. Some of the world's grandest cities and most precious cultural artifacts were lost. A significant proportion of humanity's intellectual talent was depleted. Entire communities—notably the artistically and culturally creative Jewish one in Europe—were eliminated.

The totalitarian assault was especially virulent in its degradation of the human condition. From a cultural point of view, both nazism and communism represented nothing less than the modern variants of barbarism. In both instances, the totalitarian revolutions inflicted—and did so deliberately—irreparable and immeasurable damage to mankind's cultural heritage. In this respect, the Nazis acted in Germany and in occupied Europe in a manner basically indistinguishable from the frenzied efforts of the Communists in Russia or China to wipe out the cultural attainments of the preceding generations. It is impossible to account for the churches or temples blown up, for the monuments torn down, for the library collections robbed or burned, for the artworks stolen, for other cultural heirlooms plundered or destroyed in an orgiastic atavism directed at traditional values, to say nothing of the denigration of the human spirit.

But all that pales in comparison to the cumulative toll of about 170,000,000 human beings destroyed by wars and totalitarian genocide. This estimate provides perhaps the only quantifiable dimension of the political insanity that mankind experienced during this century.

TWO

The Centrality of Metamyth

The tragedy of the twentieth century was largely unexpected. None of the predictions widely made on January 1, 1900 even came close to anticipating the ideological massacres and political warfare that followed. Yet there were inklings of what might happen even before 1900. Already in the late nineteenth century and especially by the beginning of the twentieth, conscious political life, especially in Europe, was increasingly beginning to gravitate toward, and be galvanized by, grand transcendental fictions—what I call *metamyth*—capable of activating wide support among the increasingly literate and thus politically mobilizable masses.

A grand transcendental fiction is to be understood as an irrational but compelling blend of the religious impulse to seek salvation, of the nationalistic self-identification as being superior to outsiders, and of utopian social doctrines reduced to the level of populist slogans. Permitting escape from unsatisfactory reality through a commitment to an imaginary reality yet to be achieved, metamyth served to galvanize and channel mass passions—with the spread of literacy facilitating the political appeal of the meta-

19

myths and with industrial techniques, harnessed in the name of the metamyth, making feasible the infliction of death on a scale without precedent in human history.

The appearance of metamyth as a political factor has to be understood in the context of the emergence by the twentieth century of the phenomenon of mass political awareness, that is, large-scale sensitivity to political appeals and an activist political commitment to political goals. That consciousness is a relatively recent historical development. For most of history, the masses, and particularly the peasantry, have been politically passive, largely either indifferent or bound by unquestioned traditional loyalties. Only under relatively rare circumstances—such as a challenge from an alien religion or from invaders speaking a foreign tongue or in the quite rare cases of spontaneous outbursts of peasant frustration—were the masses susceptible to activist political mobilization. Otherwise, the prevailing tendency until relatively modern times was for the vast majority of people to be politically indifferent.

The phenomenon of mass political consciousness began to make itself felt late in Europe in the eighteenth century, and continued to spread throughout the subsequent century, culminating in the explosive events of the twentieth century. Its rise can be attributed to a very large degree to three interrelated major impulses: (1) the spread of literacy; (2) the industrial revolution; and (3) urbanization. All three made themselves increasingly felt during the nineteenth century and assumed dynamic dimensions during the twentieth.

Literacy was important in shattering political passivity because it introduced, initially through pamphleteering, politically primitive masses to simple political notions, slogans, and concepts. The hitherto prevailing tabula rasa of the mass mind was suddenly exposed to concepts which seemed to strike a responsive chord: existing inequality was not an act of God to be passively accepted but a flagrant injustice; the individual, typically the peasant, was not a mere cog in a hierarchical order that was immutable, but a member of the people, or of the nation, that possessed a collective personality, rights, and aspirations. Better still, the exploited worker was not merely an urban ex-peasant but a member of a revolutionary class ordained by history to redeem humanity.

Literacy made the spread of political ideas possible. But it also meant that political ideas had to be reduced to simple notions through ideology and propaganda. This is why pamphleteering became so important in the course of the eighteenth century, especially during the French Revolution, but also subsequently during the Paris Commune and during the Bolshevik experience. All modern dictators depended on simple slogans, which provided superficially convincing but fundamentally simplistic formulas capsulating the frustrations and aspirations of the politically just-awakened masses. Lenin particularly was sensitive to the importance of simple notions and especially of hard-hitting slogans, designed to activate hatred, frustrations, and suppressed emotions. Reliance on, and exploitation of, political Manichaeanism was the expedient framework for explaining to the suddenly responsive masses the meaning of otherwise complex political reality.

It is noteworthy that mass political activism was initially confined largely to western Europe. That happens to have been the region where literacy first became a general phenomenon. By the early nineteenth century, the majority of males and about one-third of adult females in western Europe had become literate (and that was also the case in America). The rest of the world was essentially illiterate. Even at the beginning of the twentieth century in the outlying regions of Europe (that is, eastern Europe and southern Europe) male literacy amounted to only about one-third to one-half of adult males and considerably less for females.

The totals for the rest of the world were even lower, though rising very sharply.

Literacy as a key instrument of political awakening was itself a by-product of the industrial revolution, which also contributed to that awakening by drastically disrupting the social environment. The industrial process created the economic need for at least minimal literacy. Both private employers and increasingly the state itself recognized that a literate working class was necessary for the effective performance of industrial tasks. Illiterate workers could not be trained to execute more than the most routine functions, and they were thus unproductive. The gradual but accelerating sophistication of machines increasingly required manpower susceptible to quasi-professional training.

The industrial revolution had a similar impact on armies. The introduction during the nineteenth century of weapons produced by the industrial process created a need for a military manpower capable of precisely carrying out technical instructions, of executing them to the letter, and of obeying complex orders often transmitted in writing. Initially at the very minimum, the officer corps had to be totally literate; by the early nineteenth century, the NCOs had to be literate; by the early twentieth century, at least minimum literacy was required of all trained soldiers. Armies thus became also mass schools for the elimination of illiteracy.

The industrial revolution contributed to enhanced popular activism not only through the spread of literacy; mass political activism was also stimulated by spreading urbanization. For example, between the middle of the eighteenth century and the middle of the twentieth, urban population of the world increased from a mere 3 percent of the total to almost 30 percent of the total, with much of that increase initially occurring in Western Europe. That massive shift entailed nothing less than a revolution in the way of life of tens of millions of people, the uprooting of their established values and patterns of behavior. The concentration of peasants abruptly divorced from their traditional rural existence created an entirely new and restive social class. Often disoriented politically and thus susceptible to simple political appeals, the new urban mass craved—indeed, it needed—some convincing explanation for its baffling and often cruel circumstances. With religion no longer sufficing, politics stepped into the breach.

The nineteenth century can thus be said to represent the first stage in the emergence of mass political consciousness. Starting in western Europe and then gradually shifting outward, by the twentieth century that political awakening had spread to eastern Europe and to parts of the Far East. (America was a special case, for it was from the very beginning, and especially with the onset of large-scale immigration, a society composed of at least quasi-politically conscious people—that is, individuals sufficiently dissatisfied with their status quo to opt for a dramatically different life on a very distant continent.) Literacy, industrialization, and urbanization together prompted a new political consciousness just waiting to be filled with credible and politically catalytic content.

Twentieth-century metamyths eventually provided the most extreme variants of that content. But they themselves were the mixed—and certainly the perverted—offspring of doctrines and attitudes unleashed with the greatest emotional force by the impact on Europe of the French Revolution. That revolution acted as the central historical catalyst for populist political activism, animated by the newly dominant sense of nationalism, by politically assertive but romantic idealism, and by an irrational faith in the unlimited scope of "rational" social engineering. Together, nationalism, idealism, and rationalism—interacting with the spread of literacy, industrialization, and urbanization—created the brew which, when transformed, subsequently led to the monstrous metamyths of the twentieth century.

To be sure, nationalism was not simply the product of the French Revolution, but the French Revolution was the spark that ignited on a mass scale a national consciousness that was already latent by the late eighteenth century in several European countries. Particularly in France, Germany, and Poland, stirrings of national consciousness as a political manifestation were already evident during the second half of that century. In France the notion of the nation as an organic unity based on linguistic affinity was extant even earlier and by the seventeenth century had not only official standing but some degree of popular acceptance. Already in 1694, the *Dictionnaire* of *l'Académie Française* defined a nation as "tous les habitants d'un même État, d'un même pays qui vivent sous les mêmes lois et usent du même langage." Though the society was still structured on a traditionally hierarchical basis, with legitimacy vested in the monarchy, political identity in France, even considerably before the French Revolution, was thus animated by a widespread national self-consciousness that was linguistically distinctive.

In Germany during the second half of the eighteenth century, the writings of Johann Gottfried Herder struck a responsive chord in the politically divided Germany when he preached the transcendental unity of the German people—"das Volk"—and argued that man could only realize himself as a conscious member of that organic community. That community, Herder argued, was linguistically defined and had a specific personality—hence its political forms should ultimately come to reflect that unique identity through a unified nation-state.

In late eighteenth-century Poland, a belated movement for national renewal of the increasingly corrupt and impotent structure of the quasi-feudal electoral kingdom came to be personalized by Tadeusz Kościuszko—in many ways the epitome of the first modern Polish national figure. As a young professional officer who had fought against the Russian Empire's encroachments on Poland, he became captivated by America's quest for independence and even crossed the ocean to join in the effort. Subsequently returning to Poland, he galvanized the resistance to ongoing efforts by Russia, Prussia, and Austria to partition Poland. In so doing, he called on "the people" and on "the nation" to undertake drastic social reforms as the point of departure for a truly national resistance. Though defeated in battle, Kościuszko's movement helped to galvanize an initial national consciousness even among the otherwise politically passive Polish peasantry.

The defeat, in the aftermath of the French Revolution, of the Napoleonic adventures and the imposition of an essentially prerevolutionary order by the 1815 Congress of Vienna could no longer extinguish the fires set by the catalytic events of the preceding two and a half decades. National consciousness had been ignited throughout Europe, and the nineteenth century came to be dominated by the active pursuit of national aspirations which by then had become deeply rooted in a new political vocabulary and terminology derived from the experience of the French Revolution. The conservative monarchs and their supporting aristocracies—both "internationalist" or "supernationalist" or, even more accurately, "nonnationalist" in outlook—simply underestimated the latent propensity not only of the new urban dwellers but even of the peasantry to political appeals exploiting and also activating the instinctive awareness of linguistic and ethnically organic national identity.

Thus in the decades that followed, it was leaders like Giuseppe Mazzini in Italy or Lajos Kossuth in Hungary, and others elsewhere, who elaborated for their own peoples the concepts and the rationales for the individual's subordination to, and complete identification with, a new higher entity—the nation. The attainment of the nation-state—"in all its power and dominance, subordinating the individual even to the point of sacrificing himself completely," as Mazzini preached—became the obsessive goal for "Giovine Italia." The movement became the precursor and igniter of modern Italian nationalism.

Elsewhere as well a rather similar pattern became evident. For example, in Hungary, Herder's emphasis on distinctive language as the key element of shared political identity, Mazzini's movement of national rebirth, and the drama of Polish struggles for independence gave birth to Lajos Kossuth's "Young Hungary Association." It aimed at the creation of a constitutional Hungarian nation-state, one that would eschew the excesses of the Jacobins in France but would no longer be subordinate to a foreign power. It emphasized the Magyar language as a distinctive bond between a people that defined itself in one transcendent personality—the nation.

When the old, essentially conservative and prenationalist order collapsed during World War I, Europe was thus ripe for the political implementation of what by then was the decisive political orientation—the notion of the primacy of the nation-state as the basic unit of political organization and mass self-identification. That principle was then universalized in the postcolonial aftermath of World War II.

The French Revolution also was critical in injecting into the emerging European national consciousness strong doses of idealism, of faith in the unlimited scope of reason, and of a secular bias against established religion. These factors, in turn, proved to be important not only in defining the content of nineteenth-century mass political awakening but eventually during the twentieth century in perverting it into the totalitarian metamyth.

Idealism, perhaps best expressed in the writing of Jean-Jacques Rousseau, postulated the notion of a community based on harmony, conscious of its general will, and aware of its national identity. The Declaration of the Rights of Man was not only a revolutionary break with the notion of a traditional society based on a hierarchy of privilege. It defined a new concept of society, with the notion of citizenship at its core. That society was to be organized "rationally"—into equal units (or departments), with an equitable system of taxation, with a national system of education emphasizing national values, and even with an ultra-rational notion of time, expressed through a new calendar based on the decimal system.

To the extent that the church had buttressed the traditional order, its power had to be broken. Its precepts were to be replaced by the elevation of the notion of loyalty to the nation-state as the highest moral imperative. Moreover, the confident belief that "rationality"—rather than religiously defined morality—could guide political behavior generated a propensity to engage in social engineering for the sake of idealistic goals. In a paradoxical way, romantic idealism regarding the desirability of achieving a perfect society came to be linked with a dogmatic faith in the capacity of man to implement a rational blueprint for such a society.

Initially, during the first half of the nineteenth century, the effects of the new politics were, on the whole, rather benign. In his massive work on "History of Europe during the Nineteenth Century," Benedetto Croce traced the progressive spread of liberalism as the dynamic force dominating Europe's political life. Liberal revolutions were mild by nature, dominated by romantic bourgeois intellectuals, neither bloodthirsty nor fanatical. The "Spring of Nations" of 1848 was the quintessential example. But Croce also noted that increasingly the social pains produced by the industrial revolution were giving rise to the view that overcoming social injustice was a higher priority than political liberty, and that nationalism—especially after the unification of Germany—was becoming wedded to imperialism, that the exaltation of warfare was becoming the dominant theme of nationalist exhortations, and that revolutionary ethos was becoming increasingly strident.

The Paris Commune of 1871—with its collision between the "bourgeoisie" and the "proletariat"—was the signal that mass political consciousness could easily assume very bloody forms. The social tensions of urban-industrial existence were providing dramatic evidence both of the growing sense of class consciousness as well as increasingly tense class antagonisms. At the same time, the Franco-German War gave rise to an increasingly militant German nationalism. Moreover, nationalism elsewhere was fueling intensifying interstate conflicts. By the late nineteenth century, the mixture of nationalism, idealism, rationalism, and secularism was producing growing chauvinism, utopianism, dogmatism, and Manichaeanism. Each of the latter came to represent the progressive perversion of each of the former; and chauvinism, utopianism, dogmatism, and Manichaeanism combined represented the central components of the twentieth century's metamyths.

In the second decade of the twentieth century, World War I became the catalytic equivalent of the French Revolution. It smashed the traditional order that had existed since 1815, an order that on the surface at least had successfully suppressed and ignored the forces unleashed by the French Revolution. It destroyed conservative values and delegitimized the remnants of traditional authority, notably the reigning monarchies. It exalted nationalism to an extreme while aggravating already deep social tensions. No wonder then that it paved the way for doctrines that posited the notion of transcendental utopias as a salvation from earthly shortcomings.

But though World War I was a catalytic event, the preparatory work for the appeal of metamyths had been done during the second half of the nineteenth century. As noted, it was during this period that nationalism increasingly assumed the forms of chauvinism and/or imperialism; that idealism was mystified into utopian visions; that supreme confidence in rationality was transformed into dogmatic irrationality regarding human capacity to blueprint and build perfect societies; that the assault on religion produced also the rejection of moral norms as limits on political action. As a result, the nineteenth century saw the essentially aristocratic concept of personal moral responsibility for political conduct gradually supplanted by the supremacy of moral relativism in political demagogy designed to activate the masses. Liberalism and idealistic utopianism became redirected and recharged into aggressiveness and tyranny.

Both Marxism and chauvinism provided the content for the newly dominant demagogic political style. But while both came to dominate twentieth-century politics, it was Marxism that acted as the transmission belt between the idealistic emotions and the faith in rationality of the French Revolution and the later phenomenon of twentieth-century totalitarianism. Elevating the concept of revolution into a morally redemptive mission and at the same time endowing it with historical inevitability, Marxism postulated that total political control was to be the point of departure for shaping a secular utopia. That central message, articulated in the nineteenth century, then spawned its several twentieth-century offshoots: Leninism, Fascism, and Hitlerism.

The prophetic opening of Karl Marx's Communist Manifesto—"a specter is haunting Europe—the specter of communism"—within a century applied to the whole world. The Paris Commune of 1871 was followed in 1905 by the barricades of St. Petersburg, and the stage was set for the Bolshevik upheaval of 1917. But before long socialism was also contaminated by chauvinism, with the Italian socialist agitator, Benito Mussolini, emerging in the early 1920s as the prophet of fascism—the doctrine catapulting nationalism to the most extreme adulation of the state and with the state monopolizing—in keeping with the socialist legacy—central and direct economic functions. But though fascism won many adherents in interwar Europe, it was Hitlerism and Leninism that emerged as the two most powerful and destructive metamyths of the twentieth century, both dominating much of the political life of the twentieth century while causing most of the historically unprecedented megadeaths inflicted during that century.

Adolf Hitler and Vladimir Lenin synthesized into coherent and appealing wholes the various strands of political thought and, even more, of political emotion that surfaced during the preceding century and were latent in a Europe ravaged by World War I. Though the mix that each produced differed very significantly in emphasis—with Hitler's historical vision shaped by doctrines of racial hatred and Lenin's of class warfare—in the final analysis both the institutional implications and the procedural consequences of their doctrines were remarkably similar. Both Hitler and Lenin personified and preached totalitarianism, based on terror and justified by dogma. Each strove to shape a coercive utopia in the name of ideals that a century earlier had entirely different meanings. Each was a master propagandist and pamphleteer. Each was adept at depersonalizing the enemy, thereby making the act of killing into an impersonal mass production process.

Allan Bullock, in his magisterial *Hitler and Stalin* (1991), incisively compared these two pathological mass murderers as unique totalitarian leaders, but it should be noted that on the level of manipulative mass politics Hitler and Lenin were in many respects more similar—while Stalin was more reminiscent of Himmler (Hitler's Gestapo chief). The first two relied heavily on demagogy to mobilize their supporters while the latter two were organizational monsters; the former were openly bloodthirsty even in their public rhetoric, not hesitating to engage in open advocacy of terror and killings, while the latter were more secretive and even occasionally affected personal sensitivity; the former were charismatic and the latter were bureaucratic in political style.

Hitler's and Lenin's appeals fell on fertile soil. Both World War I and the growing tensions of the preceding decades predisposed many toward utopian notions. Even more critical to Hitler's and Lenin's initial triumphs was the very nature of the political consciousness on which they capitalized and which they mobilized. Given the circumstances prevailing in the early 1920s, and given the arduous nature of the context in which during the preceding decades their followers first experienced their political awakening and structured their initial political outlook, both Hitler and Lenin were able to activate a following of fanatical true believers, tapping the masses' instinctual hatreds. It is no exaggeration to characterize the outlook of their followers as highly susceptible to primitive, quasi-rational but highly emotional appeals: escapist from reality, Manichaean in explanatory terms, and extremely sophistic as well as self-righteous in attitude.

The European mind—especially in Germany after its defeat in war and also in Russia after its defeat and the revolution—was receptive to a vision of order and progress toward inevitable and socially satisfying triumph. The confused and battered populations of Germany and Russia were even more receptive to Manichaean explanations of existing turmoil and hardships—the Jews or the capitalists as the conspirators of evil, meriting total extermination. And once power was consolidated, it was only a question of time and circumstance before fanaticism was translated into genocide.

THREE

Coercive Utopia

The ultimate significance of the totalitarian experience during the twentieth century goes beyond the scale of the mortality deliberately inflicted in the name of the grand transcendental fictions so fanatically propagated. It involves the abortive attempt to coerce mankind into truly bizarre utopias. Though that attempt ultimately failed, it represented politically the most extreme and philosophically the most arrogant effort in human history to attain control over the totality of human environment, to define dogmatically mankind's social organization, and even to condition the human personality. In brief, the architects of coercive utopia allocated to themselves the role that mankind traditionally consigned to God.

To be sure, social evolution itself has involved progressively more ambitious efforts to gain control over human destiny. That quest has been pursued steadily, over the ages, with human fatalism in relationship to nature and with the spontaneous acceptance of oneself as one is gradually yielding to an increasing tendency to manipulate both nature and oneself. But on the whole, for most known and for all of unknown history, the human being has been relatively compliant toward the world around him, accepting himself as part of nature. The stark imperatives of survival were humbly borne as "natural." The basic components of social existence—procreation, family, limited cohabitation based on shared language and derived from dictates of economic expediency—were all part of an organic and spontaneous reality.

Over time, however, the cumulative learning process gradually infused mankind with an increased capacity for some degree of control over nature—initially through organized agriculture—and also gave rise to progressively more complex forms of societal organization. Step by step, humanity began to understand the seasons, to calculate the stars, to plot and to report the passage of time, and even to organize itself. Increased understanding enhanced not only the capacity for limited control but also gave rise to an enhanced thirst for understanding the mysterious world surrounding, and still dominating, human life.

The great religions—preceded by more primitive cults and various rituals of worship for the powerful forces that mankind sensed existed somewhere in the beyond (e.g., the Sun God)—thus came to serve in that context as the doctrines both of enhanced comprehension and of more sophisticated acceptance. The comprehension provided an all-inclusive explanation of the whys of human existence—the prime cause, the ultimate purpose, the final status. Relying on the incomprehensible concept of infinity as their foundation, the great religions were thus both the source of a "rational" and of an emotional grand explanation of the ultimate mystery of life.

They also served as doctrines of acceptance of the natural order of things. That acceptance could be defined, as the case may be, either as original sin, as a fatalistic resignation to a preordained pattern of life, or as withdrawal into an inner bliss. In any case, the effect was to condition mankind into acquiescence to the existential order. The real rewards of life were to come either after the end of one's physical existence or through an inward-oriented, meditative spirituality.

Broadly speaking, the rise of the great religions coincided with mankind's evolutionary growth to a stage in which humanity's transcendental questions about the meaning of life were coinciding with humanity's more organized efforts to liberate itself from a passive subordination to the vicissitudes of nature. These efforts involved more complex political systems and more coordinated attempts to cope with nature, through agriculture, irrigation, or mining. Doctrines of understanding, and of acceptance of life as primarily a spiritual experience, provided a new synthesis, giving increasingly restless mankind a framework of rules and guidelines that endured for several millennia.

That framework, however, came to be progressively diluted in the course of the modern age. The industrial revolution produced a quantum leap in mankind's capacity to challenge nature's domination of life. Secular doctrines increasingly focused attention on the centrality of earthly existence, elevating the physical human being and denigrating the spiritual dimension. Eventually even heaven on earth came to be seen as an attainable objective, provided the revealed new truth was faithfully obeyed.

This tendency assumed its most extreme form with the appearance of modern totalitarian metamyths. Both Hitlerism and Leninism-Stalinism came to usurp the role of the great religions. They did so by rejecting the latter's premises, especially by repudiating the latter's subordination of the material to the spiritual. Moreover, in actual political practice both asserted nothing less than that the totalitarian dictator was in fact the secular god: the living personalization of the infallible, all-knowing, loving and beloved, all-powerful and thus invincible, and linked to infinity by the inevitability of history. The coercively created utopia—based on the doctrines propagated by the dictator—

was to be the culmination of mankind's quest for self-liberation from nature and the mysteries beyond it, a condition of total fulfillment for the redeemed and of total rejection for the doomed.

In effect, twentieth-century totalitarianism postulated the most overreaching claim possible: that all of humanity's knowledge and all of humanity's aspirations could be compressed into a unified doctrine, based on the revealed word of a deified leader. The implementation of the metamyth through the coercive creation of a secular utopia was to be the fulfillment of history.

In retrospect, one of the great mysteries of the twentieth century must surely be how and why relatively so many intelligent and idealistic humans (not only in Germany or Russia, but throughout the world, and especially among the so-called intellectuals) could have ever taken seriously the notions of utopia propagated for them respectively by Hitler and by Lenin/Stalin. These schemes quite literally verged on the lunatic—whether the racist ravings of *Mein Kampf* or the absurdities regarding "the withering away of the state"—yet they were accepted almost as if God-given by millions of followers. It raises the troubling question of the degree to which the innately destructive and irrational side of human nature is susceptible to demagogic mobilization. The tens of millions who were killed because they were perceived, for racial or social reasons, as unworthy of living within the earthly utopia, and the many millions more who were coerced into living within these systems, testify to the hypnotic appeal of metamyths that postulated the end of history and the attainment of perfection within coercive utopias of total control.

Eventually, the coercive utopias were to become voluntary, thereby attaining the ultimate victory of doctrinal conditioning. That conditioning, in turn, was to be reinforced by the deliberate exploitation of human weakness, especially the capacity of the human being to rationalize immoral self-interest as necessary and even justified. The Bulgarian-French scholar, Tzvetan To-dorov, in his "Face à l'Extrême" (1991), a study of the impact of totalitarian terror on the human personality, noted the degree to which modern totalitarian systems took advantage of the basic human propensity to conform. Having created a mesmerizing and paralyzing impression of social unanimity, both the Nazis and the Communists demoralized their societies by encouraging mutual vigilance and mass denunciations. The goal was to make even internal resistance into a source of self-doubt, into a devia-tion that eventually the isolated dissenter was even tempted to correct.

In all the former Communist states once-secret archives which now have become available reveal that much of the dyna-mism for the mass arrests, and for many of the executions, was generated by a veritable orgy of denunciations. Such archives contain literally millions of written denunciations of neighbors by neighbors, even of relatives by relatives. This was very delib-erately encouraged as part of the process of ideological condi-tioning. In many respects, the gravest moral charge that can be leveled against twentieth-century totalitarianism is that—unlike law-governed democracies which try to constrain moral defi-ciencies and religions which aspire to elevate individual moral-ity—both the Nazis and the Communists deliberately abetted the moral deformation of the human being.

The opening of the secret Soviet archives—and also of the archives of some of the formerly Communist East European states—as well as open access to hitherto withheld socioeco-nomic statistics reveal that in fact communist totalitarianism was more criminal, more brutal, and socially more destructive than alleged by even its most severe critics. It was a system not only of mass murder—on a scale without precedent in human his-tory—but of the deliberate demoralization of society and of the reckless devastation of the physical environment. In brief, both the soul and the body of society were its victims.

The demoralization was promoted by the massive and coercive recruitment of informers. Step by step, ever wider circles of society were enlisted, seduced, or coerced into a pattern of conduct that was morally destructive and socially intimidating. Even the most intimate bonds of friendship—indeed, even of conjugal love—were not immune to the pernicious fear that one's innermost thoughts might be vulnerable to denunciation. The result was to make much of society into an accomplice of the system—as postcommunist East Europe and Russia discovered to their horror after the fall of communism.

The ethical demoralization of society—by weakening social cohesion—for a while may have made the system stronger politically. That may have been the cynical calculation of the Communist rulers who, more than anything else, wanted to preserve their power. It is difficult, however, to find an even semirational explanation for the reckless destruction of the natural environment throughout the once Communist-ruled societies. The ecological consequences of communist policies have been socially so devastating, so dangerous to the human condition—with tens of thousands of lives warped through various diseases and birth defects, and with entire regions polluted beyond recognition— that one almost is tempted to suspect that the Communist elites unconsciously viewed themselves as historically transient and thus indifferent to the fate of future generations.

A paradox was involved in this massive criminality: the effort at achieving total control produced in fact a machine of self-destruction that undermined social values and devastated the physical environment in a manner, and to a degree, such that at some point the breakdown of the system had to occur. Ultimately, the root cause of this suicidal dynamic was the morally

reprehensible notion that the utopian ends justified the application of any means—with the result that even the Communist
rulers no longer had any internalized moral guidelines capable
of defining the criteria and limits of political domination. Their
quest for total control thereby generated mindless power committed, above all, to their own self-perpetuation.

The scope of that power was to be universal. Both the Communist and the Nazi doctrines asserted their universal relevance—though in significantly different ways. The Nazi
blueprint saw the German state at the apex of a new global
hierarchy, structured on the basis of allegedly scientific genetic
laws that could identify and prioritize both the master race and
all those below it. The Communist blueprint saw the attainment
of a world revolution by the Communist vanguard as the ultimate
act of humanity's historical redemption, launching mankind into
socialism and then communism.

In both cases, history, so to speak, would end with the attainment on the world scale either of the Nazi "New Order" or of
the "Dictatorship of the Proletariat." In both cases, the coercive
creation of utopia for the chosen people (be it in Germany or in
Russia) was hence only the first stage, the point of departure,
for the transcendental transformation of the way of life of all of
humanity. The Nazis' utopia was, therefore, to have both a
domestic and an international character. The Germans, clearly
among the best educated and most civilized of the Western
Europeans, were told that their destiny was to lead the racial
purification first of Europe and then of the entire world, with
the characteristics of the ideal "Aryan type" of true German
splattered on billboards throughout the land. That few Germans
themselves—including the Führer himself—could match the
model was apparently of little concern.

German society itself was to be based on two central components: the collective "Volk" and the embodiment of the will

of that "Volk"—the "Führer." Hitler repeatedly stressed the symbiotic relationship between himself and the German "Volk": "I belong exclusively to the German people and I struggle for the German people." Exploiting the German romantic tradition, Nazi ideologues stressed that instead of the state as such, it was to be the mythical and racially pure "Volk," unified by blood and spirit, and led by its personal incarnation, that would redeem Germany from the collective ravages of defeat in World War I and from the corruption of the bourgeois-led capitalism.

Nazism, in its early domestic phase, initially had much in common with the Communist condemnation of the bourgeois-capitalist state. The founding program of 1920—"the 25 points" of the German National Socialist Workers' Party—emphasized both anticapitalism and anti-Semitism, but the movement placed special emphasis on the urgent goal of regaining for the defeated Germany its proper place in the world. Moreover, Hitler explicitly rejected the notion of equality, viewing its advocacy as a Judeo-Christian plot: "The belief in human equality is a kind of hypnotic spell exercised by world-conquering Judaism with the help of the Christian Churches." Racial hierarchy was to supersede equality, with the "Aryan race" entitled to lead. Thus Germany was to be the leader of a united but hierarchically organized Europe, with the German "Volk"—the master race—purified racially of all alien and corrupt elements. Two goals were particularly emphasized: the attainment of "living space" for Germany through territorial expansion and the elimination of the Jewish presence.

The territorially expanded Germany was to be supported by pliant satellite states in northwestern Europe and by slave colonies in eastern Europe. Consideration was also given to the creation of distant fortresslike German settlements (on the model of the Roman legions) in particularly desirable areas—such as the Crimea—to be linked with Germany by special

"Autobahns." Basically, the structure of world power was to be based on the imperial principle, with the racial factor—especially hatred for the Jews and contempt for the Slavs—defining the hierarchy.

On the symbolic level, the world's capital, Berlin, was to be reconstructed on a monumental scale, highlighting the subordination of the individual to the overwhelming power of the totalitarian leader. The plans, developed at Hitler's behest, included a new chancellery for the Führer, replacing the grandiose structure built by the Nazis in the late 1930s with a monster 70 times larger and containing an apartment for Hitler 150 times larger than Bismarck's; a building to overshadow the old Reichstag with a dome 350 meters high and with 100,000 seats for the faithful; a congress hall for 60,000 people; a sports stadium for 500,000 spectators; a marching ground for 1 million people; and a ceremonial avenue in the center of the city three times wider than the Champs-Élysées. As Hitler put it in 1939, "We must build as large as today's technical possibilities permit; we must build for eternity."

The vision of the future was historically legitimated by the Führer himself in his ultimately irrational *Mein Kampf* and by Alfred Rosenberg's pseudoscientific musings in his *Race and Race History* (or *The Myth of the Twentieth Century*). Either work justifiably raised serious questions regarding the sanity of the respective author. With one of Europe's best-educated people also compelled to greet one another in a comic fashion by a stiffly outstretched arm while loudly hailing the leader's last name, one could almost suspect that a satire had become reality. In the late twentieth century, it is almost impossible for those who have not themselves lived in the 1930s and 1940s to imagine that a modern and civilized society could have sustained such Nazi absurdities.

Unlike Hiterlism, communism did project a superficially rational blueprint for its utopia. Moreover, it was derived from an apparently idealistic impulse. But its application, pushed to an irrational degree, produced consequences that in the sheer scale of inflicted lethality was even more destructive and in moral consequences at least as repulsive. In fact, communism can be seen as the highest stage in the emergence of secular arrogance. It asserted not only the possession of the key to a totally "scientific" insight into the inner workings of the entire human experience ("a historical science") but also the vision of a state of total bliss for all of humanity (minus, of course, the exploitative classes).

In its institutional form, communism elevated the top political leader to the status of the living god, much like nazism. This worship, carried to absurd extremes in the multiple cases of Lenin, Stalin, Mao, Kim, Ceauşescu and others, led the practitioners of "scientific materialism" to the point of even worshiping the preserved and publicly displayed remains of the original founder. In that fashion mass religiosity was to be channeled into doctrinally correct secular forms.

The communist utopia was to be achieved by a combination of coercion and reeducation. While seemingly more rational than the almost comic posturing of the Nazis, the communist vision in many ways involved an even greater misunderstanding of the human personality and even more ambitious goals for reshaping that personality. Ultimately, the Nazis appealed to base instincts that did exist and exploited them to the fullest. The Communists appealed to idealized instincts and they cynically distorted them to the extreme.

The communist utopia was not spelled out in any detailed blueprint fashion either by Marx or Engels, beyond very generalized descriptions of the classless and profitless society. It was left to Lenin and Stalin actually to build it and also to conceptualize it. Lenin's contribution, cut short by his early death in 1924, focused more on the creation of the party of true believers, who acted as the personal embodiment of the proletariat especially as that proletariat was said to lack a developed class consciousness. It was Stalin's historical destiny to create the new system and to seek to define its social content.

Stalin shaped his concept of utopia through both practice and theory. The practice, broadly speaking, came first. The five-year plans, especially the collectivization and the industrialization (with the latter entailing the rapid growth of truly communal cities) were in effect stages in the process of creating a society that eventually was to be completely classless and thus truly "blissful." To achieve that utopian goal, Soviet society, to an extent considerably greater than Germany under the Nazis, was thus ravaged, destroyed (with millions murdered), and then re-built in keeping wth Stalin's basic doctrinal precepts. The system that was to emerge from this revolution from above was to be one of total control: with the individual programmed to accept political control over his personal life; with society subjected to politically controlled social engineering; and with even the laws of history subject to party control.

In the process, the cult of the leader gradually replaced the Leninist cult of the party, thereby enhancing the institutional similarities between Stalinism and Hitlerism and accelerating the process of creating a truly totalitarian system. Notably, both Stalin and Hitler shared the hubris of the divinely anointed. Stalin was quoted pontificating on every subject, be it the arts or the sciences, while his minions felt justified even in preaching to poets and musicians on what constituted correct art. Hitler, while committed to building up Germany's might, did not hesitate to deprive Germany of some of the best brains (e.g., the expulsion of Albert Einstein) on purely racial grounds.

Not long before his death, and in keeping with his exalted status as "the scientist of all scientists," Stalin attempted to articulate a program which might be considered a blueprint for the future. In his 1952 lengthy statement on "The economic problems of socialism in the USSR," Stalin assaulted both the mechanical determinism of those who argued that socialism was a reflection of a certain stage of technological development and the voluntarism of those who denied the existence of "objective laws of history." In effect, by using the "dialectic," Stalin asserted his own claim to uniquely infallible insight into the proper balance between objective and subjective forces in historical change, and then went on to sketch out his own concept of "the law of balanced development of the national economy" toward communism.

Stalin's design, though largely conceptual, seemed to augur for the later 1950s yet another phase of intense social upheaval, perhaps matching the traumas of the 1930s. Stalin's death, however, intervened and it was not until another decade passed before a new blueprint was unveiled. It came with a CPSU (Communist Party of the Soviet Union) party program, adopted in 1961, which postulated explicitly the approaching triumph of the Soviet Union in its competition with the United States. The definition of utopia was specifically focused on outperforming the most advanced capitalist state, and Stalin's successor, Nikita Khrushchev, gloried in the anticipated historical triumph.

Arguing that "communism is the bright future of all mankind," the program postulated that by 1970, even assuming that America maintained its growth rates, Soviet industrial production, by "the most conservative estimates," would exceed that of America by 5 percent, and by 1980 it would rise to 170 percent of American production. It went on boldly to assert that by 1980 the so-called socialist camp would account for 60 percent of global production, with the "imperialist camp" accounting only for less than 30 percent. All of this would mean that even in the area of living standards, the Soviet Union would surpass the

United States, "and with it will come the shortest working day, an abundance of material and cultural riches, and an even higher standard of living for all workers." In the words of academician S. Strumilin, the doctrinal interpreter of the new party program, "Imperialism is definitely embarked on a period of decline and fall." These assertions were presented as scientific findings, inherently infallible in their historical projections.

In effect, prior to the end of the twentieth century, the victory of communism was to have taken place. With the entrance of the world into the communist era, mankind was to achieve finally a state of total control in the hitherto uneasy and intellectually elusive relationship between human aspirations, societal capabilities, the natural environment, and cosmic mysteries. The ultimate dilemmas of life would therefore be resolved, through answers provided dogmatically in the context of an initially coercive but eventually voluntary utopia.

The challenge of twentieth-century totalitarianism was thus the challenge of utopian hubris carried to an extreme without parallel in history. The twentieth century was the first century of an unprecedented effort to establish total social control: to shape utopias in which history would come to stand still, in which dogmatic verities would become institutionalized under a system of rigid hierarchy, in which the redeemed would know that generations yet to come would also live in identical societal frameworks. It was a century in which man—animated by irrational metamyths—sought to usurp the divine and was cast into an apocalypse of his own making.

PART II

Beyond Political
Awakening

Does mankind learn from history? Is the political outlook of mankind, on the eve of the twenty-first century, likely to be more mature in reaction to the political madness of the twentieth century? Is a liberal-democratic consensus on a global scale now likely? And, last but not least, does the concept of a liberal democracy provide meaningful answers to the emerging new dilemmas of social existence?

One could certainly argue that the failure of nazism and of communism sets the stage for a global embrace of the political ideas unleashed more than two hundred years ago by the American and French revolutions. Their hopeful assumptions regarding human nature and the political organization of society have not been invalidated by the perversions inherent in twentieth-century totalitarianism. The example set by the actual experience of democratic America, Europe, and Japan speaks for itself. It should not only reinforce the lessons that ought to be extracted from the failure of the totalitarian challenge, but it should also enhance the appeal of the liberal democratic concept itself.

It is also possible, however, that in fact the notion of a historically conditioned learning process is an illusion, especially when critically examined in the global context. A strong case can be made that the twentieth century was the last century in which global affairs were shaped largely by European concerns and dominated by events originating in Europe. Viewed in this light, even the bitterest totalitarian crimes can be perceived as by-products of a specifically European history—with its special proclivity to chauvinism, doctrinal fanaticism, and preoccupation with utopian as well as Manichaean political solutions. The failure of these cumulative tendencies should not be, therefore, perceived as the automatic confirmation of the universal validity of the alternative liberal democratic outlook.

The French historian Jean-Marie Domenach has noted correctly that in applauding the failure of Marxism, Westerners have not fully grasped the fact that they may be saluting the last Western attempt to rationalize and universalize history. One is, therefore, justified in suspecting that the disappearance of communism might conceivably produce altogether different consequences in such areas as North Africa, or South Asia, or Latin America. And with the end of Western universalism, there is also a further risk: that the combination of political liberalism with the growing social hedonism in the West is more likely to generate sheer envy elsewhere than affirmative democratic commitment.

The question as to what will be the intellectual legacy of the totalitarian era is of decisive importance for the future stability of the global political system. That system today contains, for the first time in history, a population that is truly politically awakened. That is a decisively important new reality. It makes for a basic historical discontinuity from the era in which political awareness was confined largely to Europe—not long ago the political center of global power—and to remote North America.

The political awakening of mankind in Asia, Latin America,

and Africa is a consequence of processes that represent essentially an extension of the European experience, discussed earlier. As in Europe, the worldwide spread of literacy and the increasing urbanization of the populations have been of decisive importance. And enhancing their impact is the added factor of new global communications, which intensifies political consciousness through a new sense of proximity, especially with its intimate awareness of existing inequities.

Even as recently as 150 years ago, communications were still preindustrial, with time and distance impeding the spread of a wider sense of nationhood and of common political vocations. In that respect even western Europe was still in the same age as agrarian Asia. In 1840 only England had a railroad system that linked its major cities (but it did not extend either into Wales or Scotland). On the Continent itself, only several capitals (Paris, Brussels, Berlin, Vienna, and Budapest) had short rail lines extending to what today would be considered suburbs. But change came quickly. By 1850 rails extended into Scotland, and on the Continent a network appeared, linking Paris, Brussels, Amsterdam, Berlin, Warsaw, Budapest, and Vienna. By 1880, western Europe was covered by a spiderweb of links that extended all the way to St. Petersburg. Political ideas as well as national troops could thus move rapidly.

The late twentieth century equivalent is the sudden appearance in the last two decades of a worldwide network of telephone communications, the appearance of global television, the introduction of the revolutionary faxing process. The effect has been to eliminate barriers to audial and visual communication. Worldwide access to radios and TV has been growing exponentially. In 1965, the BBC estimated that there were some 530 million portable radios in the world; by 1990, their number had grown to 2.1 billion. During the same period, the total number of TVs had grown from 180 million to over 1 billion. And even more politically significant is the fact that whereas in 1965 about 80 percent of the foregoing were located in North America and Europe, by 1990 that share had declined to only about 55 percent of the much larger total. Ideas have now a worldwide instant reach and immediate impact.

Their political grasp is magnified by the continued and accelerated spread of literacy, the necessary precondition for mass political activism. Literacy levels outside of western Europe and North America were still relatively low in the beginning decades of the twentieth century. UNESCO and other studies indicate that in southern and eastern parts of Europe the rates were only somewhere in the 30-percent range; in Egypt and India under 10 percent, and in Latin America around 50 percent. By the middle of this century, they had jumped to over 70 percent in southeastern Europe, doubled in Egypt and India, and grown to about 70 percent in Latin America. The process accelerated even more rapidly in the second half of this century, making most of mankind accessible and susceptible to political pamphleteering.

The collapse of worldwide but Europe-centered empires was obviously accelerated by World War II, but it probably would not have happened so rapidly without the politically galvanizing impact of the spread of literacy. Access to the written word made possible more support for the conspiratorial and then agitational anticolonialist political action. It provided the platform for the emergence of charismatic populist leaders who articulated and channeled awakening mass political passions. It facilitated large-scale political mobilization even before World War II. For example, in China—where political action hitherto had been primarily a student manifestation—already by 1925 the Chinese Kuomintang had succeeded in recruiting some 600,000 political activists, while by 1929–30 the Chinese Communists had five provinces with some 30 million people under direct political tutelage. The

Congress Party of India in a similar fashion galvanized heretofore politically passive masses.

The global spread of literacy has coincided with the acceleration of urbanization in the developing countries. Whereas only about 17 percent of their populations lived in urban centers in 1950, by 1990 the total had doubled to 34 percent, with projections indicating that by 2025 the figure will be around 60 percent. The majority of the poor people in the world will thus be concentrated in urban slums, uprooted from their traditional rural environment; they will be literate, and they will be susceptible to political mobilization.

To compound the likely pressures, these masses will also be much more numerous. The actual numbers of people involved—given the high rates of population growth in most Third World countries—are almost staggering. Thus in 1950 the urban population of the less developed countries came to about 285 million; by 1990, the number had exploded to a total of 1,385 million. And within less than twenty years, by the year 2010, that total is expected to double, to about 2.7 billion! (In contrast, the urban population of the developed parts of the world is projected to grow only from 876 million in 1990 to about 1 billion by 2010.)

A congested and intimate global political community, characterized by rising levels of political awareness, is thus emerging, but it is emerging in the context of continued and, in some respects, even widening socioeconomic disparities. As a consequence, these vast, newly politically activated masses are in the process of experiencing a compressed historical progression in the subtle relationship between political outlook and social conditions. In the earlier agricultural societies, patriarchy, hereditary authority, and tradition together defined the framework of life for illiterate and passive masses, with revealed truth of the great religions providing the answer to the ultimate questions that every thinking human being at some point ponders. In increasingly urban-industrial societies, the thirst of more literate masses for political explanations and for political correction of their condition unleashed doctrinal passions and generated a search for secular utopias. In the emerging postindustrial technetronic societies, the emphasis is on pragmatism, information, democracy, as well as philosophical skepticism, politically institutionalized on the basis of relative social well-being and insulated psychologically from the relatively poor parts of the world.

The danger on the eve of the twenty-first century is not only that these several states of development in political awareness are coexisting and clashing on the global level; it is that the politically activated masses outside of the rich, largely Western democracies are predominantly in the first phase of this awareness. Typically, that first stage is characterized by a narrowly defined political self-identity based to a high degree on ethnic exclusiveness. The public mood, therefore, still tends to be expressed through primitive ideas, susceptible to Manichaean appeals—both religious and political—and often also escapist and self-righteous in their propounded solutions. The very notion of the complexity of the social condition is alien to that mode of thought, and so is the political practice of compromise. The old Leninist slogan, "Who is not with us is against us," can be appropriately redefined here as meaning "Who is not us is against us."

That primitive first stage of political awakening manifested itself throughout the Third World following its post–World War II emancipation. Leaders such as Sukarno, Nkrumah, Mobutu, or even Mao (despite his doctrinal pretensions) came to epitomize the politics of personal passion and brute power, in a setting of obsequious cults of the personality as vulgar and demeaning as those of Hitler and Stalin. Under them, political processes became both corrupt and violent, economic policies became increasingly irrational, and the overall political atmosphere poisoned by intolerance and doctrinal or ethnic prejudice.

However, such instinctive xenophobia has not been an exclusive Third World phenomenon. The economically more vulnerable classes in the developed world are susceptible to it as well. With migratory pressures creating a large presence of East Europeans and North Africans in Western Europe competing for jobs, and seemingly threatening the established way of life of the poorer urban West Europeans, ethnic xenophobia has been spreading through France, Germany, Belgium and other countries of even the rich and democratic West Europe. The French National Front in early 1992 in some polls enjoyed the support on the immigration question of as many as 38 percent of the French. The German Skinheads similarly reflected, through violent acts against foreigners, the philosophy that "who is not us is against us."

A distinctive aspect of the contemporary global political awakening is that it is taking place in a philosophical context largely bereft of any deeper commitments. Apart from the Islamic world, where fundamentalist political tendencies are quite marked, the global political scene is dominated by rhetoric and values that are primarily consumption oriented and that stress personal self-gratification as the primary purpose of political action. The influence of the life-style of the advanced Western countries, as projected by global television, is especially decisive in that regard, shaping a worldwide preoccupation with the acquisition of material goods and with the instant satisfaction of morally uninhibited personal desires.

In earlier phases of political history, the initial phases of mass political awakening tended to be much influenced, first by religion, and later by ideology. On the one hand, that gave the suddenly politically awakened a strong moral compass for determining what was right and what was wrong, and for defining priorities other than the purely material. But on the other hand, these true (but also simplistic) believers were inclined to express their intense commitment through violent intolerance, persecutions, and even genocide. In that respect, the fading of religious fanaticism and the more recent failure of ideological utopianism represent a process of maturation, perhaps giving the phenomenon of global political awakening a more benign flavor.

At the same time, however, there is the risk in the current emphasis on cornucopian goals of a moral confusion that could become susceptible to a new wave of irrationality and escapism, driven by the sense of deprivation vis-à-vis the very visibly richer life-styles of the advanced Western countries—and also on the part of the poorer people toward the rich within the advanced countries themselves. The waning in the latter of deeper spiritual content means that their primary message to the poorer and more recently politically activated global masses is to stimulate their desire for material emulation—which, however, as a practical matter—even with the most reasonable socioeconomic policies—is simply unattainable for most of the world's deprived. The message of material emulation thus unintentionally becomes the catalyst for frustrated but unstructured envy, which in turn could be easily manipulated by demagogic extremists.

The result is the global crisis of the spirit. Enduring tenets of faith are replaced by fashionable slogans while comprehensive doctrines give way to vague yearnings. The fall of communism thus raises the question of whether its defeat is tantamount to the victory of democracy in a comprehensive, systematic, and endemic way.

Indeed, how certain can one be that "proper" lessons are actually being drawn from the political experience of the waning century? Will the new political participants draw the same lessons that are being drawn by the largely American and European victors in the century-long conflict between totalitarian and democratic concepts? Much depends on how that contest comes to be assessed by the nonparticipants in it—but much also depends on the degree to which the victorious contestants succeed in projecting their own historically successful global political outlook.

The above questions suggest concern that the defeat of the totalitarian challenge may not yield a new universal consensus, based on an updated synthesis of the democratic ideals articulated most fully in the course of the French and American revolutions. Instead, it might produce new and quite dangerous dichotomies in outlook, derived both from culturally as well as economically different contexts, dramatized by different levels of technological and economic development, all of which intensify gaps in perspective and aspirations.

ONE

The Victory of Small Beliefs

In reflecting on the future, it is appropriate to take as one's point of departure the potentially controversial proposition that coercive utopia was not defeated by some alternative unified grand vision. Rather, its defeat was largely derived from its own fundamental misconceptions. Those coerced into it, as well as those fearing its spread, shared in common certain basic but largely inchoate human instincts that were in direct contradiction with its utopian assumptions and its transcendental arrogance.

As noted earlier, the communist utopia represented intellectually a more substantial challenge than the Nazi. Though both produced similar political consequences, the Nazi utopia was founded on irrationality, emotion, and racial-ethnic hatred. Its "Aryan" appeal was inherently self-limiting. Its eventual success had to depend on military prowess—and its defeat in war automatically meant the end of the phenomenon itself.

The communist appeal was more complex and more engaging. It drew heavily on the intellectual legacy of the early nineteenth-century utopian thinking, stimulated by the twin impacts of the French (political) and the industrial (economic) revolu-

tions. It reached out to those who were appalled by the disloca-
tions and inequities of capitalism in the early industrial age. It
resuscitated old Christian prejudices against private property,
expressed so strongly and as recently as the sixteenth century in
Thomas More's *Utopia* (in which private property and the central
role of money were perceived as precluding justice and social
well-being).

Ultimately, communism failed because in practice it did not
deliver on the material level while its political practices compro-
mised—indeed, discredited—its moral claims. It could not provide a viable socioeconomic alternative to the free market system
that in the meantime had adapted some socialist concerns as its
own social (even if not economic) policy. In effect, as a practical
matter, it can be said that capitalism defeated communism by
depriving it of its monopolistic claim to morality while simply
outperforming it on the material plane. It thus rebutted the
grandiose assertion of communism to be mankind's highest stage
of development.

Communism—born out of a moral outrage—by rejecting enduring spiritual values and by reducing morality to an instrument
of politics, made its own success dependent entirely on material
performance. And here it could not deliver because it misjudged
the nature of human creativity and especially the very nature of
the human being. It could not harness human potential because
it crushed the human spirit. The critical connection between
creativity and the acquisition of wealth was grossly misunder-
stood. It severed the umbilical cord between productivity and
self-interest. The suppression of private property produced economic lethargy and eventually systemic underperformance.

Moreover, the totalitarian system that was created in its name
in the Soviet Union not only stifled initiative and innovation
but could not assimilate the need inherent in the postindustrial
society for decentralized mass communications and for the spon-

taneous interaction of freely flowing information and multiple centers of decision making. At the same time, the assault on the spiritual dimension of life had the effect of focusing primary attention on the system's material performance—exactly the area of the system's operational weakness. The moral fervor that initially drew some to communism was thus eventually dissipated, but without compensatory material gratification.

As a consequence, communism's dogmatic self-righteousness reduced idealism to barbaric inhumanity and to institutionalized hypocrisy. It pushed its claim to rationality to an irrationally dogmatic degree even while claiming the actual attainment of utopia in the face of massive evidence to the contrary. The two together—the perverted idealism and the dogmatism masquerading as rationality—created the destructive flight from reality. The resulting inability to cope with the realities of the modern technological age ultimately spelled the historic doom of communism.

Thus of the four central components of the French Revolution—rationality, idealism, nationalism, and secularism—nazism adopted, adapted, and finally distorted to the extreme nationalism and secularism, while communism—seemingly embracing all but nationalism—in practice became the antithesis of the progressive ideas unleashed some two hundred years ago. It failed to create "the new man" and the social utopia that would condition him. Instead, it imprisoned "the old man" in a failed social experiment.

Twentieth-century metamyths were thus grandiose in their appeal but weak in application. In contrast, the enduring human instincts, the thirst for some spiritual self-expression, the basic verities of daily life, and the practical requirements of the information revolution all conspired to sustain an internal awareness of an alternative for those coercively incorporated into the utopias. Indeed, that awareness generated even highly idealized notions of what life was actually like outside the totalitarian systems.

Eventually, it was the cumulative and often petty frustrations of daily life that were in fact critical in undermining the viability of communist utopia. It was the regularity of the encounters with brutal functionaries, the endless queuing for badly made and rarely available consumer goods, the increasingly grating confrontations between official slogans and official hypocrisy, the mindless humiliations and dehumanization of life inherent in the subordination of society to a bureaucratized hierarchy, the contrasts between the embarrassing shortages of even elementary items (such as toilet paper) and the thinly camouflaged lifestyle of the totalitarian rulers that progressively turned conviction, submission, apathy, and fear into repudiation, revulsion, and restless activism.

By the same token, it follows (alas!) that coercive utopia would almost certainly have endured much longer, perhaps well into the next century, had it succeeded in gratifying mankind's minimal material aspirations. Human nature being what it is, many under the totalitarian regimes were resigned to living in quiet submission. To be sure, the failings and the irritations of the system would have continued to generate opposition—led by heroic and self-sacrificial dissidents—but it is unlikely that such opposition, even in the setting of growing moral revulsion, could have overthrown the coercive totalitarian machinery if it had been reinforced by relative material success. Though it may sound cynical, Barrington Moore, Jr. was probably right when he asserted in his 1989 lecture at Columbia University that:

> In general, people have not wanted democracy for its own sake or out of commitment to a political ideal. For the most part those who have actively sought democracy—in the literal sense of rule by the populace—have wanted it as a device to increase

their share in political rule and weaken the power and authority of those who actually rule. Democracy has been a weapon of the poor and the many against the few and the well-to-do ever since it surfaced in ancient Athens. The liberal component, where it has existed, was an attempt to gain protection against arbitrary acts by *either* the poor and many, or the dominant few. (Italics in the original.)

It was not, therefore, some grand and integrated mobilizing vision of democracy that undermined, sapped, and eventually drained communism of its vigor. Rather, it was a combination of repressed religious aspirations, of basic human libertarian instincts, of some liberal notions, and of many daily and practical encounters with an official reality that defied both reason and simple common sense, that cumulatively created the circumstances that led to the sudden and surprisingly peaceful implosion of communism both as a system and as a doctrine.

The defeat of communism was thus partially—but very partially—the victory of the democratic idea, of the free market system, of religion, and of nationalism. Each element played a role—indeed, an important role—but not a single one of them was the decisive, unifying, and mobilizing factor. Rather, instinctive reactions, shared but whispered confidences, internalized religious feelings, offended national sentiments coalesced into a generalized repudiation of the coercive utopia.

To assert the above is not to denigrate either the heroic role of some individuals nor to deny the historic function of alternative and more ambitious religious or political philosophies. Both were important agents of change—be it Lech Walesa and Vaclav Havel or the Catholic church or the concept of democracy. Nor is it to neglect the vital—indeed, uniquely important—role played by the United States in deterring Soviet military expansion and in raising high the standard of human rights.

But once communist expansion was contained, the underlying struggle was waged on the daily level, with communism increasingly colliding with instinctive individual awareness of some fundamental human rights and with the ordinary desire for a "normal," more spontaneous, and also materially more gratifying existence. And, ultimately, even the lethal combination of the worst of ideology with the worst of technology—the totalitarian formula for the twentieth century—could not prevail over these uncrystallized yet powerful personal beliefs.

However, a warning is in order at this stage: lacking any integrative structure, small beliefs can easily degenerate into petty vices. A personal democratic instinct is not the same as a democratic political culture. It can also be the point of departure for quarrelsome politics. The instinctive moral rejection of repression, and especially of petty bureaucracy, is not yet the same as the adoption of compromise as the basic political principle, the acceptance of complex constitutional arrangements, and especially respect for a sovereign judicial system. To this day, there is unfortunately little recognition of—and respect for—the complexity and sensitivity of the democratic process in most of the former communist countries and in particular practically none in the former Soviet Union.

The case is similar with respect to the free market. On the personal level, the rejection of statism reflected primarily a frustration with the overly bureaucratized system of imposed deprivation. Increasingly, the social benefits of communism, such as cheap housing or other social entitlements, were dismissed because they came to be outweighed by the physical discomforts. But it does not follow that the publics in the former communist countries, despite their verbal adoption of the rhetoric of the free market, partake of the operational culture of capitalism. The evocation of the word "market" (and one hears the word "rynok" over and over again in the former Soviet Union) is not a substitute for internalizing entrepreneurial behavior, for grasping the financial complexities of the banking system, and for recognizing the extremely subtle difference between private initiative and individual greed.

One can go on and speak also of religion in this context. The denial of freedom of worship produced widespread resentment. But individual resentment is not the same as the social acceptance of religion as a binding system of moral rules that determine individual behavior. It is doubtful that any of the former communist countries will become what might be considered a truly religious society. In fact, in those former communist countries in which the church played a major role in mobilizing effective opposition to communist oppression, the liberation from communism has produced in its wake a significant decline in the appeal of established religion. The church, once the asylum of free thought, in some places seems also to be seeking authority that infringes on the freedom of conscience and expression.

The defeat of communism's coercive utopia thus contains both a promise and a danger. The promise is inherent in the impulses that led to its repudiation and failure. If the promise can be tapped, then perhaps the stage might be set for a global synthesis of the democratic ideas unleashed with such compelling force in America and France some two hundred years ago. But the inchoate state of the prevailing political outlooks in the ex-communist states, and especially the lack of integration between such potentially conflicting impulses as the religious, nationalist, and secular-materialist could produce a condition in which the small personal beliefs that so effectively opposed the communist metamyth could first degenerate into unrealistic expectations of materialist self-gratification and then turn—out of sheer frustration and anger—into new doctrines of hate.

TWO

Permissive Cornucopia

A great deal depends here on how the advanced West reacts to the disappearance of the communist ideological challenge. Will the values of the pluralistic and free market societies strike a viable balance between individual desire for material self-enhancement and the need to infuse into life an awareness of its transcendental dimensions? The dilemma was posed well by Nobel laureate Czesław Miłosz, who wrote in mid-1991 that:

> Marxism always seemed to me to be a consequence of the profound erosion of man's religious imagination on the European continent. Dostoevsky understood this when, in *The Possessed*, he depicted in prophetic shorthand the actions of revolutionaries engaged in an attempt to give meaning to history in a world without God. In this sense, totalitarian movements had a metaphysical background stamped with a minus sign, and can be counted among the manifestations of "European nihilism." The erosion of the religious imagination is, in my view, the core of twentieth-century thought; and it is what has lent our age its apocalyptic features. But the dissolution of totalitarian move-

ments by no means suggests that a fundamental change has taken place in this regard. It is enough to look at the prosperous and well-fed sector of humanity in the countries of the West to become convinced that the concept of a religiously ordered cosmos is disintegrating also under the impact of science and technology, and that if people, especially among the younger generations, still have a strong need for faith, it is a homeless, groping faith that does not necessarily turn to Christianity.

The warning expressed by Miłosz points to the historic danger that the discredited metamyths of coercive utopia might be followed by the spiritual emptiness of permissive cornucopia. The very word "cornucopia" is derived from the mythological horn that suckled the god Zeus. It has the miraculous capacity to become full of whatever its owner desires. The term "permissive cornucopia" can hence be applied to a society in which everything is permitted and everything can be had.

There are some grounds for serious and legitimate concern that in the advanced, rich, and politically democratic societies cornucopian permissiveness is increasingly dominating and defining both the content and the goals of individual existence. The notion of a "permissive cornucopia" involves essentially a society in which the progressive decline in the centrality of moral criteria is matched by heightened preoccupation with material and sensual self-gratification. Unlike coercive utopia, permissive cornucopia does not envisage a timeless state of societal bliss for the redeemed but focuses largely on the immediate satisfaction of individual desires, in a setting in which individual and collective hedonism becomes the dominant motive for behavior. The combination of the erosion of moral criteria in defining personal conduct with the emphasis on material goods results both in permissiveness on the level of action and in material greed on the level of motivation. "Greed is good"—the battle cry of the

American yuppies of the late 1980s—is a fitting motto for permissive cornucopia.

The corruption inherent in permissive cornucopia is not only the consequence of existential abundance. It can also be the result of the absence or denial of such abundance in the eyes of the growing number of those who are aware (by television or sheer proximity) of its existence but feel personally deprived of its privileges. The economic travails of the West, with the growing number of unemployed and even of the permanently excluded (such as a significant portion of blacks in America), create the condition of militant desire for the fruits of cornucopia as well as of a more pervasive inclination to reject moral restraints on any—even violent—"get-rich-quick" schemes.

The advanced West today is the model for the social aspirations of the shipwrecks of communism and of the deprived masses of the Third World. To be sure, the philosophical and cultural content of the West is in flux, and perhaps to define it as permissive cornucopia is too severe a judgment. Many exceptions can be made. And we can reserve for later a more specific discussion of the state of American society, especially as it bears on America's capacity to exercise a decisively important global role. For the moment, *suffice it to say that if in fact the predominant Western culture and the West's preponderant philosophical outlook do reflect values that justify the cornucopian appellation or values that arise out of the feeling of cornucopian denial, concern would be justified both regarding the long-term viability of the so-called Western civilization and especially its capacity to provide a meaningful message to the politically awakened world in the post-utopian phase.*

As originally conceived, Utopia—the imaginary island of Thomas More—was to be a voluntary association of people living in a state of political and social perfection, reflecting the goodness and altruism said to be inherent in human nature. The very idea of the island of perfection implied a self-contained existence, not contaminated by the impurities of the human condition at large. Modern totalitarians perverted the idea in two significant ways: utopia was to be established by force, and coercive utopia was to be the nuclear component of a worldwide upheaval.

Permissive cornucopia is almost its polar opposite. A notional society capable of providing almost magical satisfaction of individual yearnings has no need for coercion. It can be permissive—indeed, it has to be permissive—for in a cornucopian society all wants can be met, and met on a highly individualized basis. Since all desires can be satisfied, all are thus also equally good. It follows that neither coercion nor self-denial is necessary. But a society in which self-gratification is the norm is also a society in which there are no longer any criteria for making moral judgments. One feels entitled to have what one wants, whether or not one is worthy. Thus, moral judgments become dispensable. There is no need to differentiate between "right" and "wrong." Instead, for pragmatic reasons of social order, the critical distinction is between what is "legal" and "illegal"; thus legal procedure, especially the court system, substitutes for morality and for the church as the principal definer of that morality. Religion as the internalized guide to individual conduct is thus replaced by the legal system, which defines the external limits of the impermissible but not of the immoral.

One can call the foregoing "procedural morality," based on external rules guiding conduct and social interaction. It differs fundamentally from a morality that is internalized, personal, and inclined to make distinctions between "right" and "wrong." Moreover, procedural morality—if it stands by itself—tends to create a condition in which more than just a few are tempted to test pragmatically the limits of the permissible—"to try to get away with it"—because no absolute inner moral restraint is operational. It becomes largely a matter of judging how effective, or ineffective, is the procedural system of restraint, and then of acting accordingly. Some tendencies in contemporary America seem to point in that direction. The several celebrated accounts of Wall Street financial scandals, or the emergence of an organized drug subculture, or widespread street crime provide good illustrations of the social consequences of this proclivity. Self-restraint gives way to violence and self-control is replaced by corruption.

Under ideal circumstances, in a law-respecting democracy, procedural morality and inner morality would be mutually reinforcing. The delicate balance between them would rest on the social acceptance of the sovereignty of judicial procedures and on the state's acceptance of the existential desirability of social institutions dedicated to the reinforcement of internal, personal morality. In the past, that latter role was largely played by organized religion. But in modern society, both politics and economics conspire to create a culture inimical to the preservation of an important social domain reserved for the religious. An increasingly permissive culture, exploiting the principle of the separation of church and state, squeezes out the religious factor but without substituting for it any secular "categorical imperatives," thereby transforming the inner moral code into a vacuum.

That moral vacuum defines the essential meaning of the notion of spiritual emptiness—an emptiness which appears to be increasingly pervasive in much of what is called Western civilization. It is a striking paradox that the greatest victory for the proposition that "God is dead" has occurred not in the Marxist-dominated states, which politically propagated atheism, but in Western liberal democratic societies, which have culturally nurtured moral apathy. In the latter, the fact is that religion has ceased to be a major social force. But this condition arose not because officially propagated atheism had won the day over religion, but because of the corrosive effects of cultural indifference to anything but the immediately and materially satisfying dimensions of life.

Two other issues of major importance are pertinent here: the definition of freedom and the definition of the good life. The first pertains to the meaning of citizenship and the second to the essence of the human being. In a society that culturally emphasizes the maximization of individual satisfactions and the minimization of moral restraints, civic freedom tends to be elevated into a self-validating absolute. *In other words, civic freedom is divorced from a notion of civic responsibility.* Traditionally, since both the French and the American revolutions, the notion of freedom was defined in the context of citizenship: that is, a definition of individual rights within a sociopolitical setting which involved also some responsibilities to that setting. However, for these responsibilities to be voluntarily shouldered genuine motivation is required, which in turn calls for an inner spirit that prompts the willingness to serve, to sacrifice, and to exercise self-restraint. Patriotic citizenship was the framework for the definition of civic freedom within a democratic society.

This definition today is in jeopardy. Increasingly, freedom is defined as the accumulation of rights and entitlements as well as license for any form of self-expression and gratification. The notion of self-imposed or socially expected service to society has become unfashionable. Thus, in effect, personal freedom becomes the absence of restraint except in cases of legally defined threats to someone else's physical or material well-being.

The gradual redefinition of freedom, away from the notion of responsible civic freedom and toward the notion of licentious personal liberty, both contributes to and is reinforced by ongoing trends in mass media. On the whole, the values conveyed by the media repeatedly manifest what justifiably might be called moral corruption and cultural decadence. Television is a particularly

serious offender in this respect. Today, for much of the world—
and especially for the young—television is the most important
instrument both for socialization and education. In that respect,
it is rapidly replacing the roles traditionally played by the family,
by the church, by the school.

Television gives the young viewer a first glimpse of the outside
world. It first defines—and does so compellingly, by combining
the visual and the audio impact—the meaning of the good life.
It sets the standards of what is to be considered achievement,
fulfillment, good taste, and proper conduct. It conditions desires,
defines aspirations and expectations, and draws the line between
acceptable and unacceptable behavior. With audiences around
the world increasingly glued to television sets, there is nothing
comparable, either in the era of enforced religious orthodoxy or
even at the high point of totalitarian indoctrination, to the cultural and philosophical conditioning that television exercises on
the viewers.

It is a staggering fact that, according to data from Nielsen
Media Services, an American housewife spends twenty-eight
hours and thirteen minutes per week—or about one-quarter
of her waking hours!—watching television, and that American
teenagers do so for about twenty hours a week. Even more
appalling are the data accumulated by the Educational Testing
Service, which indicate that the proportion of children aged
thirteen who watch television for five hours or more per day—
or upwards of thirty-five hours per week!—is over 20 percent
in America, and somewhere in the range of over 10 percent for
both Western and some developing countries. Even the lower
percentiles underline the importance of television in shaping
perceptions and values.

The content of American and West European television has
been under much discussion. Not all of it is undesirable; some
of it occasionally is even good. But Gresham's Law applies not

only to good and bad money; it applies also to programming that is exclusively dependent on advertising and audience appeal. The sad fact is that television producers who are cultural pornographers have in effect a competitive advantage over those who are not. The net result is that Western television has become progressively more and more inclined to the sensual, sexual, and sensational. Even a single day's test of the content of the "sitcoms" that dominate daily viewing, and of much of the evening entertainment, not to speak of the advertisements themselves, conveys the foregoing with intense impact.

Moreover, to the extent that any values can be extrapolated from television programming, they clearly extol self-gratification, they normalize intense violence and brutality, they encourage sexual promiscuity through example and stimulated peer pressures (advertisements for condoms addressed to American teenagers and children describe potential customers as sexually "active"—with the obvious negative inference that the others are "inactive") and they pander to the worst public instincts. The result is loss of control over social behavior.

This indictment is especially applicable to the widely viewed global exports of American television and of the American film industry. "Dallas" and "Dynasty" have been shown in more than one hundred countries, and the image that they present of American values is not likely to reinforce America's global standing. On the contrary, while the distorted picture of American wealth may be envied, the overriding vulgarity and spiritual emptiness which these images of America project reinforce skepticism that America has a deeper message to offer to the contemporary world. American movies in recent years have also come to be dominated by brutish violence and physical and sexual savagery, with growing box-office rewards for each surpassing dose of abominations. It is no exaggeration to say that Hollywood movie and TV producers have become cultural subverters

who—cynically exploiting the shield offered by the First Amendment—have been propagating a self-destructive social ethic.

The foregoing is directly relevant to the definition of the
essence of the good life. Increasingly, it is defined by television—
the prevailing purveyor of mass culture—as the acquisition of
goods and instant self-gratification more generally. The utopian
fanatic is in this fashion replaced by the insatiable consumer. In
the age of awareness of massive human inequity and deprivation,
it is politically and morally disturbing to calculate how much of
Western consumption is unnecessary: that is, driven by artificially stimulated desires for the latest fads, fashions, gimmicks,
and toys. Moreover, consumption derived from artificially induced desire and not from need is increasingly a middle-class
phenomenon, not just confined to the very rich. But the very
rich—usually the newly very rich—do set the style, and their
vulgar and conspicuous consumption contributes to an atmosphere in which material consumption—derived not from want
but from self-gratification—becomes the decisive equivalent of
the good life.

The morally corrupt definition of the good life is not only
projected by television. The standard is also set by what the
public tends to view as "high society," the glittering social sets
of New York City and Los Angeles, dominated by wealthy corpo-
rate executives, investment dealers, real estate speculators, and
mass media moguls. Their extravagance, though lampooned by
some social critics (e.g., Tom Wolfe), is presented in magazines
and on the social pages of newspapers as glamorous while their
greed is often extolled as a measure of their professional acuity.
The accolades that greeted the entry of the late Robert Maxwell
onto the New York City social scene were but a singular reflection of this cornucopian debasement of values.

Indeed, consumption patterns in the West confirm the economic law postulated by the nineteenth-century French political

economist, Jean-Baptiste Say, that supply creates its own demand. And that demand can get out of control, especially if continuously and deliberately stimulated by the cultural context. To be sure, demand also stimulates economic growth, and the diffusion of prosperity—not only within the West but eventually also on a global scale—is dependent on continued expansion of economic productivity. The issue, therefore, is not the fact of demand or even of its desirability—it is of its content and direction. The choice—and the associated dilemma—were crisply defined in Pope John Paul II's social encyclical "On the Hundredth Anniversary of Rerum Novarum" ("Centesimus Annus," 1991): "It is not wrong to want to live better; what is wrong is a style of life which is presumed to be better when it is directed towards 'having' rather than 'being,' and which wants to have more, not in order to be more but in order to spend life in enjoyment *as an end in itself*" (italics added).

Without some criteria of judgment that are derived from internalized standards, the political danger is that self-gratification is becoming an end in itself in the West at a time when much of the rest of the world is still struggling with existential needs. At a time when the two worlds are no longer separated by time and distance, it is disturbing to note how much of Western consumption is in fact unattainable by the poorer majorities of mankind. If, by some miracle, these majorities were to acquire the cars, the Frigidaires, the air conditioners, the microwave ovens, as well as the myriad of other gadgets that define the well-being of the richer peoples, the world's economy and its ecology would be overwhelmed. Intensified envy rather than successful imitation is the more likely prospect.

A related danger arises from the economic advice that the West proffers to the newly emancipated victims of communism. With communist utopianism discredited, some in the West have been advocating a new utopianism of their own, a procedural utopianism that champions a particular economic process without any regard for moral consequences. In its extreme form, this has expressed itself through unqualified advocacy of the free market mechanism, presenting it as almost an automatic source of salvation from the pernicious legacy of communism. In its disregard of the absence in some of the former communist states of any social safety nets, such advocacy thus smacks of the Darwinian notion of survival of the fittest. As a result, the attempt to establish a free market in some places is assuming forms reminiscent of the nineteenth century, colliding with elementary notions of social justice. It may prove difficult for the postcommunist countries—given their dire economic conditions—to make the kind of social welfare adjustments that the free market system has successfully undertaken in the West. This is already weakening the appeal of Western-type democracy itself.

To sum up, coercive utopia was an attempt at total control. It was based on the misguided notion that a political system could define the totality of life, condition the individual completely, and legitimate a system of permanent rule by those with a mysterious insight—through their dogma—into the meaning of life. Permissive cornucopia creates the illusion that one's life is under control, through the self-deceptive assumption that self-gratification is the exercise of control. In fact, it creates a condition in which the dynamic escalation of desire for sensual and material pleasure becomes the dominant cultural reality. Morally infused choice becomes irrelevant. In the context of worldwide political awakening and of the simultaneous reality of massive socioeconomic disparities, the foregoing hardly foreshadows the emergence of a globally shared and unifying political ethic.

THREE

Philosophical Polarization

These cornucopian trends, which threaten to become dominant in the culture of the West, give rise to a politically critical consideration: does the West have a vision, a set of values, and a way of life that offers a relevant guide to the future for the politically awakened mankind?

Democracy may be the West's central contribution, but democracy is a vessel that has to be filled with content. The democratic political process, the constitutional system, the sovereignty of law are all peerless guarantees for the preservation and enhancement of individual rights and of human personality. But democracy by itself does not provide the answers to the dilemmas of social existence and especially to the definition of the good life. That role is played by culture and philosophy—which together generate the values that motivate and shape social behavior.

The concern already expressed—namely, that a meaningful social model for the politically awakened globe cannot emanate from permissive cornucopia—is accentuated by the diverse impact of modern science on the global human condition. In the technologically and economically advanced parts of the world, science and technology are dramatically enhancing the human capacity not only for self-gratification but also for self-alteration. In poorer portions of the world, modern communications intensify the awareness of global injustice on the part of the masses preoccupied with the struggle for their own physical survival. In the context of global intimacy, a dangerous gap in fundamental concerns is thus widening.

The developing or poorer world, concentrated largely in the Southern Hemisphere and embracing the enormous majority of mankind that resides in China, southern Asia, Africa, and portions of Latin America, confronts a continuing demographic explosion, rapid but chaotic urbanization, massive poverty, high infant mortality, and relatively short life spans, not to speak of periodic epidemics, famines, and general deprivation. Modern science is being used to address some of these hardships, and progress in coping with epidemics and in enhancing agricultural production has been notable during this century. There also exists now both an international machinery and the technological capacity for quick aid and for concentrated responses by various relief agencies to the most grievous crises.

The most important political effect of technological innovation has been to create social intimacy on the global scale—overcoming time and distance. But that new intimacy both combines and collides at the same time. In much of the world, the daily struggle for survival by the acutely impoverished masses now occurs in the context of an intense awareness of a totally contrasting life-style on the part of its own elites as well as of the cornucopian West (with which the elites of the poor countries identify themselves and which they aspire to imitate). *As a result, for mankind the gap between enhanced expectations and actual capabilities may have never been as great as it is today.*

Furthermore, in the advanced world science increasingly creates a dynamic toward human self-engineering which may soon become as uncontrolled as the dynamic of self-gratification. In fact, self-alteration is in part self-gratification. In the absence of any deliberately defined criteria of choice, self-alteration may become as massive as the technological and scientific onslaught on the natural environment that is already occurring. The ecological movement, in response to that assault, has been seeking to define some criteria of self-restraint so as to preserve the organic balance between humanity and nature. In doing so, it has been attempting to gain control over a dynamic process in which human domination over nature created the illusion of control by the former over the latter while in reality mindlessly destroying the organic connection between the two. This is why the ecological movement, in its root assumptions, is more of a philosophical than political emanation.

An analogous dilemma is now surfacing with regard to human self-alteration. Inherent in the illusion of enhanced human self-control through science is the urgent surfacing of questions that are of ultimate importance: What is the human being? What is the irreducible and essential quality of human authenticity?

These issues are likely to become dominant questions in the advanced countries within the next several decades. The industrial revolution has led in this century to the temptation and the illusion that social engineering, based on a dogmatic ideology, can produce collective well-being within arrogantly coercive utopias. More recently, the revolution in science has given human beings the ability to destroy society in its entirety. Now a revolution in science is creating the prospect that human beings will be able to tamper with themselves through biotechnological and genetic engineering. This will have profound ethical and philosophical implications for the world.

The practice of human organ transplants, for example, has

steadily increased. Today, surgeons can already replace limbs, ears, joints, and even hearts with man-made substitutes and are a decade away from doing the same with artificial kidneys and pancreases. Some speculate that it is only a question of time before it may even be possible to transplant a brain from one body to another. Such a procedure will raise directly the question of where the identity of a person resides. Harvard philosopher Robert Nozick, in his book *Philosophical Explanations*, has puzzled on the meaning of personal identity through time, focusing primarily on the implications involved in the transfer of memories and character from one body to another. In effect, questions that were formerly reserved for academic departments of philosophy may soon be posed for society at large.

At the same time, science is making great strides in the development of artificial intelligence. Today's computers are essentially limited to performing difficult and complex calculations, but tomorrow's may have powers rivaling those of the human brain. Scientists involved in developing artificial intelligence are basically recapitulating with machines the evolutionary process that created intelligence in humans over the millennia. In the future, instead of doing tasks, computers will be thinking through problems; instead of analyzing data, they will be reasoning through to solutions; instead of *processing*, they will be *creating*. Science is also on the threshold of creating experience-assimilating robots. And it is a very real possibility that in the not-so-distant future, computers may actually be, so to speak, conscious—that is, cognizant of goals and of the world around them and of their place in it.

All of this is bound to push to the forefront key questions which the cornucopian culture tends to slight. What are the frontiers of the authentic uniqueness of the human being? What is the interrelationship between the philosophical and the physical, and how is that interrelationship achieved and integrated within a single human being? What are the criteria for defining a good society, perhaps first on a national but eventually on a global scale?

These are simultaneously political as well as philosophical issues. Already, in the most advanced Western societies, the question that is generating the greatest passion increasingly is less and less "ideological" in the nineteenth-century systemic sense and more and more philosophic-scientific in essence. When does life begin? How does one define "life"? Who has the right and the "knowledge" to make that determination—a priest, a philosopher, or a scientist? And who has the right to decide whether to terminate that "life"? A mother, a doctor, the state, or the church? These questions pertaining to the politically divisive issue of abortion thus blend religion, philosophy, science, and politics. And all of them apply to euthanasia as well, likely to become the next large social dilemma.

Genetic engineering in particular is already beginning to pose quandaries that before long will make the ideological battles of the twentieth century seem intellectually primitive, and that could divide mankind even more sharply than has hitherto been the case into the privileged and the deprived. Scientists are already advanced in the effort to decode the one hundred thousand genes which contain the blueprint for the human being's organic existence from fetus to death. Some predict success in the global effort, called the Human Genome Project, within fifteen years or so. Not only will genetic forecasting thus be possible, genetic engineering is already underway. A significant start has already been made in animal husbandry, improving the quality of leaner meat and protecting animals from birth from such diseases as cancer. It is inevitable that the effort to protect against disease will be applied to human beings as well, starting first with genetic screening and then expanding to genetic engineering. The results could be revolutionary for human life to a degree without precedent in all of mankind's history.

In the absence of any moral criteria of restraint, there is the danger that the dynamic of genetic engineering could develop a momentum of its own. External self-gratification would thus come to be matched by self-engineering. In a society largely unguided by moral or philosophical criteria, the process could become dominated by selfish aspirations and exploited by those with the means to take advantage of it. Despite the efforts of some within the scientific community to set self-controlling standards, the expanding power to reshape human life may thus come to be exercised without any defined guidelines.

It is likely that genetic enhancement both of intelligence and of physical attributes will be primarily available—at least for some time—to the privileged of the world. In effect, a new and dramatic gap may soon open up in the human condition. Indeed, one can reasonably speculate that genetic engineering to improve human intellectual capabilities and physical health will in all likelihood at some point become initially accessible only to the most powerful and the richest elite of the most advanced countries (and perhaps to a few of their counterparts in the poorer countries). A new and truly divisive cleavage between the genetically enhanced and others (in some ways dangerously reminiscent of Hitler's racial musings) might thereby emerge.

Inherent in the foregoing is the potential for dramatic dichotomies not only in global social concerns and capabilities but also in basic political concepts. They foreshadow the danger—especially to the newly politically awakened of the world and even to the richer societies—that the political philosophy of liberal democracy could cease to be a relevant and intellectually guiding framework for coping with the most gripping human issues. This could lead to intensified philosophical confusion and political conflicts, with mankind's cultural condition polarized at the extremes: on the axis of deprivation versus gratification. *In history's arena, the challenge of the utopian fanatic could thus yield to the clash between the insatiable consumer and the starving spectator.*

In any case, in the advanced world, the frontiers of science are likely to be pushed to the extreme, enhancing for some the external and internal dimensions of life to a degree that will amount almost to the transformation of the very character of human existence. One must hope that in the more distant future, in reaction to the spiritual emptiness of modern cornucopia and the new challenges of science, modern society may begin to refocus on the significance of the philosophic and even spiritual facets of life. Out of such concern there could arise eventually a greater preoccupation with the definition of socially binding moral criteria for harnessing the awesome power that humanity is increasingly acquiring and mistakenly thinks it is commanding. Though a return to the traditional centrality of institutionalized and formal religion in mankind's social life is highly unlikely, renewed respect for man's spiritual well-being may then provide the point of departure for some assertion of morally infused control over the dynamics of historic change.

This would be in keeping with Vaclav Havel's eloquent call for a philosophical redefinition of modernity—that is, of the age of the worship of "reason" initiated by the French Revolution. As he put it in early 1992:

> Man's attitude to the world must be radically changed. We have to abandon the arrogant belief that the world is merely a puzzle to be solved, a machine with instructions for use waiting to be discovered, a body of information to be fed into a computer in the hope that, sooner or later, it will spit out a universal solution.

It is my profound conviction that we have to release from the
sphere of private whim such forces as a natural, unique and
unrepeatable experience of the world, an elementary sense of
justice, the ability to see things as others do, a sense of transcendental responsibility, archetypal wisdom, good taste, courage,
compassion and faith in the importance of particular measures
that do not aspire to be a universal key to salvation. Such forces
must be rehabilitated.

Perhaps such a postmodern redefinition will eventually occur,
though the practical political consequences of any such redefinition are difficult to divine. But the rethinking is beginning to be
felt in philosophical and scientific discussions. Some academic
thinkers are inclined to reject the emphasis placed in the modern
age on the notions of scientific certainty and uniformity; they
emphasize instead the reality of contingency and diversity. For
example, Jean-François Loytard, in his *The Post Modern Condition—A Report on Knowledge*, stresses the importance of the cata-
strophic and of the paradoxical in scientific inquiry, challenging
the notion that knowledge points to certainty and uniformity.

In the meantime, on the more superficial level of political
attitudes, changes in global political outlooks are likely to point
in contradictory directions. In the postcommunist world, the
pains of the transition to capitalism may well undermine the
appeal of the democratic ethic. In that setting, there may be
greater proclivity to take refuge in more organic and more tightly
binding beliefs such as ethnicity, xenophobia, or religion, perhaps fueled by disappointment with, and contempt for, the "corrupt and selfish West."

In the disunited but socially frustrated former Third World
of southern Asia, Africa, and elsewhere, envy and resentment of
the global elites residing in the Northern Hemisphere—and of
their homegrown, West-imitating and hence culturally deraci-

nated counterparts—could produce intensified political passions, susceptible to mobilization by any well-organized state prepared to undertake the mission of global redemption. However, the mobilizing quest for "equality" and "justice," colliding through global communications with the new and more complex dilemmas of the advanced societies, is likely to lack the doctrinal cohesion of the ideologies of a simpler age and is thus likely to express itself through a variety of ideological caricatures.

To sum up, in the advanced world personal issues increasingly dominate politics and hedonistic concerns shape social life, while science opens up altogether new prospects for individual self-enhancement; in the poorer parts of the world, basic concerns with survival and passions of frustration characterize social and political existence, while modern communications enhance mass awareness of the existing global disparities. Thus neither the failure of utopianism nor the worldwide political awakening yet signals the emergence of a global political consensus.

PART III

The Peerless Global Power

In the final decade of the twentieth century the position of America in world affairs is paradoxical. On the one hand, the United States is perched on top of the world. It faces no rivals capable of matching its comprehensive global power, power that has four dimensions to it: 1. global military reach; 2. global economic impact; 3. global cultural-ideological appeal; and, cumulatively as a result of the foregoing, 4. global political muscle. On the other hand, the dynamics of America's social change as well as the value content of the American message to the world threaten to undermine America's special role as the global leader.

Currently, no other state even comes close to matching the United States in global prestige and power. Russia still has the nuclear arsenal of a superpower but does not have the ability to project its forces worldwide, while its large conventional army is demoralized and disintegrating. In other aspects, Russian power is altogether deficient. Germany and Japan have economic power, but it is not clear that either one of them could soon translate economic into political-military power. A unified Europe could do so only if a major leap forward in the process of European unification generated a single political-military entity.

In contrast, America possesses not only overwhelming strategic power—constantly enhanced by technological innovation—but also an unmatched capability to project its conventional forces to distant areas. For the world at large, one of the most impressive aspects of the U.S. military performance in the Gulf War of 1991 was the manner in which the United States was able to deploy, and logistically sustain, a force of several hundred thousand men in the distant Arabian peninsula. This unique military capability is supported by an economy that is still the world's largest, and that has retained its relative share of the global GNP at a level of approximately 25–30 percent for much of this century (except for the much higher levels during the brief and unique decade after World War II). This combination, in turn, gives the United States a worldwide political influence that no other nation can even approach.

No wonder then that a CNN/Angus Reid Group poll—taken in mid-1992 in Europe, Asia, and Latin America—indicated that America is not only viewed as currently the world's leading state but that most people in the world expect America to remain so into the foreseeable future. This is not only a matter of physical power. In the present phase of history, American emphasis on personal rights is also a major factor in determining America's unique standing. Earlier, the French Revolution—as already noted—had a galvanizing impact on France's European neighbors. It triggered the utopian notions that so dominated the politics of the nineteenth and twentieth centuries. Today, it is America—with its political freedom and its mass culture—that is impacting on a world which modern communications have made so much more intimate.

However, in a world of rapid change, one must also ask: Can America sustain its special position over the long haul? Are there rivals on the horizon that might actually displace America? (For example, about 20 percent of the respondents to the poll just cited above did say that by the end of the century Japan might emerge as America's successor.) And, on a broader level, to what extent are the values and the realities of contemporary America relevant to a highly differentiated world undergoing a massive political awakening? Indeed, what is the cultural content of the American message to the rest of the world?

History teaches that a superpower cannot long remain dominant unless it projects—with a measure of self-righteous confidence—a message of worldwide relevance. That was the experience of Rome, of France, and of Great Britain. *But unless that message is derived from an inner moral code of its own, defining a shared standard of conduct as an example for others, national self-righteousness can degenerate into national vanity, devoid of wider appeal. It will be eventually rejected by others—as was very much the case with the fall of the Soviet empire. This is why the internal dynamics—not only economic but especially cultural—of contemporary America are so directly relevant to America's capacity to influence constructively the thrust of global change.*

Changes in the character of international politics, changes that increasingly blur the traditional distinctions between international and domestic politics, further magnify the relevance of America's domestic condition to America's global standing. An appreciation of the nature and implications of that change is the necessary point of departure for an assessment of America's own staying power as the globe's currently preeminent state as well as of the actual prospects of any possible future rivals to America's preeminence.

ONE

The Paradox
of Global Power

This century was dominated by three great struggles for global preponderance: between Germany and the Franco-British entente; between Germany and Japan and the United States and the USSR; and finally between the United States and the USSR. In that respect, the twentieth century was internationally much more turbulent than the nineteenth—which, following Napoleon's defeat, was relatively stable, with the British Empire acting as the decisive arbiter of power within a relatively conservative world system.

However, the end of the third great struggle between the United States and the USSR coincides with the surfacing of a basic transformation in the nature of international politics. That transformation, progressively accelerating under the impact of modern economics and communications, involves the dilution of the primacy of the nation-state and the emergence of a much more intimate connection between domestic as well as global economics and politics. Increasingly, world affairs are shaped by domestic trends that recognize no frontiers and require collective responses by governments less and less able to act in a "sovereign" fashion.

This process is not receptive to dogmatic ideological formulations which—as was the case throughout much of the twentieth century—divided the world into "good" and "evil" social systems. In fact, it is marked by an increasing tendency toward ideological homogenization, with a bureaucratically controlled and supranational capitalism becoming the universal social system. In that world, bureaucratic and financial connections that cut across frontiers, reinforced by political trends increasingly influenced by transnational mass media, are gradually rendering irrelevant the more traditional notions of exclusive state "sovereignty."

As a consequence of these new economic and social realities, a global political process is emerging. It is both transforming and replacing traditional international politics. And in that process, America is not only the key player, but a player whose internal structure and dynamics make it organically congenial to that emerging process. America's openness to outside participation in its own affairs—through foreign-sponsored lobbies, growing foreign ownership of its assets, and even some foreign participation in the definition of its domestic agendas—makes America both the exemplar and the harbinger of the increasingly porous definition of the nation-state. At the same time, that reality also reinforces the American proclivity to view the world as part of a common political process, with America entitled to be engaged in the domestic affairs of other states, dispensing sometimes even irritating judgments regarding their economic priorities or human rights.

Inherent in the appearance of this still rather shapeless global political process is the shaping of an initial worldwide consensus that might be the beginning of a universal moral standard. Its

essence has been aptly summarized by Professor Ralph Buultjens (in *Ethics and International Affairs*, vol. 6, 1992):

> Connected to and also independent of human rights concerns
> is another process—the globalizing of political morality. . . . The
> result is the construction of a body of international ethics whose
> putative custodian is an amorphous but real entity known as the
> world community. The features and the character of this entity
> are presently blurred, but that it has an expanding power of
> collective sanction is not in doubt. Expressions of disapproval,
> provoked by political behavior unacceptable to a nascent morality,
> sometimes have a sharp physical bite—the governments of South
> Africa, Iraq, and Haiti are among those who have felt it. Thus,
> conceptual abstractions, grounded in widening common under-
> standings, are occasionally able to summon powerful agents of
> enforcement. As the personality of the world community becomes
> more clearly sculpted, a development which is not yet assured,
> its capacity for intervention could increase—foreshadowing more
> future intrusions that will seek to alter the pattern of behavior of
> nations.

The coincidence of the worldwide mass political awakening
and the current democratization of domestic politics in parts of
Asia, Latin America, and the former Soviet bloc very much
encourage this transformation. Democratic politics are, by definition, open. With the growing impact of mass communications
transcending national frontiers, the democratic processes of individual countries are becoming more and more susceptible to
the impact of ideas, and even personalities, that are of external
origin. Almost all democratic political parties are also members
of various "international" coalitions, thereby cross-fertilizing
one another and blurring further the traditional international
dividing lines.

However, the world, despite the emerging reality of an increasingly common global political process, is still divided into leaders and followers. The pace and style of political change is set by what might be called the catalytic nations, radiating their influence to their immediate neighbors, prompting also imitation among the more distant, and leaving only a few isolated regions impervious to the impact of new political fashions and ideas. The physical and psychological intimacy of the modern world both accelerates and enhances the impact of such catalytic nations.

France played the role of the catalytic nation for much of the modern age. The French Revolution set in motion, then exemplified, the concept of the nation-state that percolated throughout the subsequent two centuries. Even Napoleon, the terminator of the revolutionary phase within France itself, was the disseminator of the new notions of politics throughout Europe, blending in different ways, depending on the setting, the components of idealism, nationalism, and secularism.

France thereby became the first catalytic nation-state, acting as the agent of history, transforming others by the force of the ideas that it had set in motion. Even the relatively more remote European peripheries became susceptible to its radiating influence, which provoked imitation as well as adaptation of the French political rhetoric and institutions. The new organization of the state—with "the citizen" as its basic unit and with more or less equally sized "prefectures" (or districts)—was much influenced by the French inclination to logic and symmetry. In the process, the state itself, speaking officially through a single national language, became the embodiment of the nation.

During this phase in mankind's political history, the state thus became the central "sovereign" unit of world affairs. These affairs, in turn, were dominated by the most powerful units, notably the Europe-based empires. Throughout much of the nineteenth century, Great Britain was the most important player, exercising a balancing role in order to prevent the emergence of a single globally dominant state, while itself the prime force in world economics and finance. In 1880, for example, Europe accounted for more than 61 percent of the world's manufacturing output, with Great Britain alone accounting for 23 percent of the total (while the United States accounted for less than 15 percent). British economic-financial prowess and control over the oceans permitted London to exercise decisive influence on the power politics of the day. As a result, the global pecking order was clear, but in a setting of an essentially conservative interstate system, in which the role of Great Britain was that of providing needed equilibrium.

The rise of America to world preeminence during the twentieth century has coincided with the crisis and then collapse of the relatively conservative world order, based on a hierarchy of sovereign states. Indeed, by the end of the century the once-evocative concept of exclusive state sovereignty has come to be displaced by the much more popular notion of inclusive international interdependence. This shift in emphasis reflects the surfacing of the new global political process, with its blurring of the distinction between the truly foreign and the exclusively domestic.

Within this global process, it is America that today is the genuinely catalytic nation—the object of admiration, resentment, imitation, and—even more dramatic—of immediate and intimate impact on the social mores of other nations. America dominates the global chatter, the global perceptions, and the global educational interactions. At any one point more than five hundred thousand foreign students (with close to two hundred thousand of them from Asia) are studying in the United States (which is several times more than at any other host country). It has been estimated that more than 80 percent of the global transmission and processing of data originates from America, that more than 50 percent of the worldwide film viewing involves American-made productions (and even more so of TV "sitcoms"). No nation comes even remotely close to the United States in the dissemination of television programming abroad. (In recent years, the UK and France have been in second place, but though each country traditionally has had worldwide cultural aspirations, their respective sales have amounted to less than 15 percent of the total American export hours.) Every continent is thereby affected (some would say, infected) by the images and values which American TV projects. This condition has prompted frequent foreign charges that American "cultural imperialism" has become a threat to indigenous cultural diversity.

Moreover, America is, in fact, itself a global society in microcosm. Its open multiculturalism—with New York a semi-European metropolis, Miami a quasi-Latin American city, and Los Angeles rapidly becoming an extension of the Orient—reinforces the organic links between America and the rest of the world. Even America's urban-racial turbulence mirrors the more unsettled social and philosophical condition of the world at large, while internal American trends are not only the objects of foreign fascination but are perceived as forecasts—for good or bad—of their own futures.

Foreign imitation of America is now a worldwide phenomenon. This is not only a matter of cultural fashions, social styles, or patterns of consumption. It also manifests itself in politics, both on the serious and on the trivial levels. The growing worldwide sensitivity to human rights, though in part the inevitable consequence of the global political awakening, has been intensified by America's emphasis on the issue. The rather adversarial relationship of the American mass media toward the government, and especially the role played by investigative political journalism, has generated earnest foreign imitation. The style of personal campaigns for top executive offices has been increasingly patterned on American presidential elections. Most important of all, the widening recognition of the centrality of stable and respected constitutions as the legitimate framework for national politics has been influenced by the uniquely enduring role played by the U.S. Constitution within such an otherwise rapidly changing society.

Underlying all of this has been America's association, since its very inception, with the notion of personal freedom. That association has made America not only a catalytic nation but a magnetic polity, attracting millions throughout its history—as it still does today. Moreover, this magnetic attraction also has stimulated intensifying pressures elsewhere for the adoption of bills of rights and of other guarantees of individually free political self-expression.

Imitation also has extended to the formal as well as trivial aspects of political life—but these, too, provide examples of the catalytic role exercised currently by America. More and more states—ranging from postcommunist Russia to the Far East—are adopting into their governmental structures an organ called the "NSC" (National Security Council)—explicitly modeled and even named after the U.S. version because of the mysterious glamour with which the press has surrounded that particular agency of the U.S. president. Similarly, more and more states have copied U.S. military uniforms, seeing in them—as was earlier the case with the French and the British—the models of their own martial future. Even the manners and the appearance of the Secret Service that protects the U.S. president have been assiduously copied abroad!

These admittedly superficial examples are a reflection of a deeper reality: the context and style of international politics are set by nations that, at different stages of history, reflect in their conduct, organization, and ethos the emerging future. For a brief period of time—and for a much more limited segment of humanity, and to a much larger degree through the application of coercion—the Soviet Union was also seen as such a force. Its example, both on the serious and also on the superficial levels, was imitated throughout the communist world. Be it a matter of the Politburo's role as the chief decision-making organ, or of Soviet-style uniforms, not to speak of socialist realism in culture, it was the Soviet Union that briefly, and in the end unsuccessfully, aspired to the role of the world-class catalytic state.

Today, America plays that role, largely to an undisputed degree. Just as earlier France stimulated the emergence of the nation-state as the principal unit of world affairs, and in a much more conservative age the British Empire was on top of a global hierarchy of such states, today America is propagating, by its own presence, the emergence of a much more comprehensive and organically interdependent global political process. It does so in a context in which world politics are increasingly mirrored in its own domestic politics, and in which its domestic politics are suggestive of global politics in microcosm.

The consequence of this condition produces a paradox. On one level, America today is the only state that possesses all the four decisive attributes of a global superpower. Yet, at the same time, America is shaping a pioneering new pattern of global politics, the inherent characteristic of which is not only the progressive dilution of the sovereign integrity of the nation-state but also the reduction in the capacity of a superstate to exercise decisive global power.

In effect, America's global preeminence reinforces and even generates the conditions that prompt America's increasing global impotence. It is a striking fact that the power of the United States in the world is analogous to that of the U.S. president in coping with America's various domestic, especially racial/urban problems. The president is expected by many to be able to act decisively, though in fact his power is limited not only constitutionally but also by the very complexity of the problems that he confronts, and especially by the democratization that galvanizes more and more demanding constituencies. Their entitlements become their rights, and expanding rights inherently become obstacles to the exercise of power.

A similar condition prevails worldwide. Global political problems are simultaneously socioeconomic, environmental, and even philosophical. They are thus less and less susceptible to clearly defined answers, and even less so to the application of military power emanating from a single political center. Demands of the poorer states for greater equality, at least of opportunity, are becoming entitlements. International institutions—even such as the World Bank or the IMF, not to speak of the specialized and functional UN organs—are becoming increasingly independent of decisive American influence as they become themselves more assertive sources of decision making.

Two examples from recent history illustrate the limitations of America's superpower status, limitations inherent in the emergence of the new global political process. At the Rio de Janeiro conference on the environment (held in June 1992), the United States was not able to fashion a coalition of the richer states in support of its own rather conservative position and, as a result, found itself outside of the new global consensus regarding the primacy of ecological concerns. American power was insufficient to sustain the American position.

The other example pertains to U.S. leadership in the Gulf War of 1991. The American military performance was spectacular. Yet to wage the war, the United States had to solicit financial and political support from a coalition that did not fully share the American sense of moral outrage regarding Saddam Hussein and which in turn was able to limit the military scope and the political aims of the war. (This condition even led one leading

Japanese international affairs scholar—quoted in the *Japan Digest Forum* of May 9, 1991—to declare that "the U.S. does not have a comprehensive ability to be the world's policeman. America should humbly recognize this.") As a result, the U.S. military victory did not become a decisive political triumph but rather a partial success as well as a continued and inconclusive embroilment. The outcome in Iraq stood in sharp contrast to the outcome of the earlier military action in Panama, where American power was unconstrained locally and not dependent on international support.

American preponderance, in the setting of the evolving global political process, therefore has a different meaning, and lesser practical consequence, than is suggested by the notion of America as the only superpower within the new world order. That world "order," however, is yet to emerge, though a global hierarchy of power exists, though America is at the top of that hierarchy, and though America is today the principal catalytic nation. Instead, at hand is a global organic process cutting across national frontiers and producing global politics that are less susceptible to neat definitions and clear-cut power arrangements.

It is a process that at one time contained the promise of greater global cooperation—yet at the present time threatens to become gridlocked, messy, and perhaps even violent. While the world does not favor anarchy as such—for most states realize its destructive potential—and while the once-fashionable appeal of "revolution" has become discredited by the failure of communism, such a world is more inclined to deny legitimacy to any single power, even if globally the most powerful.

In that context, U.S. preponderance is both a reality and an illusion. Everything—especially in the area of international security—ultimately depends on the American response. Yet that response, as is clearly the case within U.S. domestic politics, is inherently circumscribed not only by the sheer scope of the interlocking dilemmas facing the politically awakened global community but also by the fact that *American global power is not the same thing as American global authority.*

Authentic authority has the advantage over power in that a lesser level of energy is required in order to exercise it—because compliance tends to be almost automatic. But compliance to authority is derived from the perception of legitimacy, based in turn on shared values. The messy global political process, to a far greater extent than the conservative international system of the past, demands such unifying values, if global cooperation rather than conflict is to become its principal reality.

The relevance of American values to what might eventually be called a new world order thus becomes the essential question. There is no doubt that America emits a compelling and appealing message of liberty to the world. However, much of the message is procedural, with its emphasis on a constitutional process that guarantees human rights and freedom of choice. Yet just as important is the social and cultural content of the American message—the mores and life-styles that it disseminates. Unless these are historically relevant, the danger arises that American global power—if deprived of the needed legitimacy and thereby lacking the capacity to assert positive control— could be undermined by the global impact of America's own values.

TWO

The Dissonant Message

In years past, when America seemed so far away, separated by vast oceans, the American message of liberty defined in very broad relief the global perception of that nation. When the world started shrinking but was also simultaneously threatened by the totalitarian challenge, the defense of freedom defined America to much of the world. With the totalitarian challenge successfully rebuffed and with the world now shrunk to the level of instant visibility, immediate communication, and growing intimacy, it is the reality of American life and the actual values of American society that increasingly define America to the rest of the world. And a close-up perception of American society as it actually is, and not in its idealized form, tends to yield increasingly ambivalent and even critical reactions.

American global leadership, and especially American authority, is thus bound to become more dependent on what actually transpires within America—on how the American economy copes with the competitive challenge of its foreign rivals, on how America defines in practice and in its values the meaning of the good life, and on how America responds—on the basis of the foregoing—to the concrete dilemmas of the politically awakened, postutopian world. The American response can either serve to deepen or to bridge the conceptual dichotomy between the cravings of the newly activated masses in what used to be called the Third World as well as the former Soviet bloc and the cornucopian culture of the post–Cold War victors.

Contemporary America—critically scrutinized to an unprecedented degree by the rest of the world—currently faces a series of tangible and intangible challenges. The response to the tangible ones will most probably be of decisive importance in defining America's relationship to its economic power rivals, especially Europe and Japan. The response to the intangible ones will be even more decisively important in shaping America's broader capacity to exercise genuine global authority—*that is, to transform its power into a leadership that commands moral legitimacy.*

Any checklist of America's shortcomings or domestic challenges is bound to be arbitrary and selective. Nonetheless, the list that follows probably includes the main problems or dilemmas currently besetting America. Approximately the first half of the list can be considered as involving what might be called "hard" issues—more susceptible to correction by concrete actions or governmental policies—and the second half requiring attitudinal shifts before an improvement can occur (with both halves obviously overlapping). The former also impact more directly on economic performance, while the latter affect and reflect more generally the values and culture of society, though also indirectly bearing on the economy.

The list is not in order of importance, but to the extent possible, it tries to deal with the items in a relational sequence. The twenty basic dilemmas requiring some degree of redress constitute, in effect, the agenda for America's renewal and for the effective reaffirmation of America's capacity to exercise sustained global leadership:

1. *Indebtedness*—which has already generated a cumulative national debt in excess of $4 trillion, which involves a budget deficit in the neighborhood of some $400 billion in 1992, and which imposes an increasingly critical—potentially even devastating—burden on America's future;

2. *Trade deficit*—which forces America to borrow, with America already the world's leading debtor nation, and which threatens some key sectors of production and employment, and which thus contributes to unemployment;

3. *Low savings and investment*—which are in part encouraged by a tax system which favors special interests as well as encourages consumption but not investment, with the result that both savings and investment rates are significantly lower than those of America's principal economic rivals, and which in turn is generating a relative decline in America's global lead in research and development;

4. *Industrial noncompetitiveness*—which, despite some signs of recovery even in the afflicted auto industry, is aggravated by the absence of any long-term national target setting (in contrast to both Europe and Japan), not to mention the disruptive effects of leveraged buyouts;

5. *Low productivity growth rates*—which, despite still relatively higher American levels, have been rising more slowly than in the case of America's principal rivals; and which are further adversely affected by higher levels of labor unrest and strikes and a declining work ethic;

6. *Inadequate health care*—which, despite the enormous sums actually spent on American health, still leaves tens of millions of Americans without adequate care and which produces life expectancy rates considerably lower and infant mortality rates higher than those of the leading European nations and Japan;

7. *Poor-quality secondary education*—which, again, despite relatively higher spending in terms of the percentage of GNP, leaves

American youth badly uneducated as compared to most European and Japanese teenagers, and which results in some 23 million American adults being functionally illiterate;

8. *Deteriorating social infrastructure and widespread urban decay*—which applies to the majority of the large American cities, with urban slums of a kind extant only in the poorest Third World countries, not to speak of a highway system, including bridges, in need of major repairs, a practically nonexistent fast-rail transportation system, as well as inadequate sewage, dams, and other facets of modern social infrastructure;

9. *A greedy wealthy class*—which tends to oppose genuinely progressive taxation (even though the most affluent fifth accounted in 1991 for 46.5 percent of all income, while the poorest fifth accounted for only 3.8 percent of all income); which in some egregious cases is quite prepared to practice massive illegality in an effort to enrich itself (e.g., the vivid account in the 1991 bestseller *The Den of Thieves*); and which involves too many CEOs of publicly owned companies insisting on remuneration—often carefully shielded from stockholder scrutiny—at levels several times higher than either in Western Europe or Japan;

10. *A truly parasitic obsession with litigation*—unmatched in the world (with more than one-third of the world's lawyers practicing in the United States), with the costs of the tort system consuming about 3 percent of America's GNP (or three times more than among America's principal rivals) and with an incalculably inhibiting effect on entrepreneurship;

11. *A deepening race and poverty problem*—with the shameful total of 32.7 percent of all black Americans living (according to the 1992 Census Bureau report) below the poverty line—one of every three!—but with also 11.3 percent of white Americans similarly afflicted, combining for a total of 35.7 million Americans (including several million helplessly homeless) living in conditions unworthy of "the peerless global power";

12. *Widespread crime and violence*—which is partially the product of the foregoing (with the black 12 percent of the national population accounting for almost 50 percent of all prison inmates) but which is made worse by the extraordinarily easy access to lethal weaponry, with more guns in private hands—and even actually in criminal hands—than in most armies around the world. With a TV and film culture that extols violence, all of this produces the highest rate of homicide of any civilized country in the world;

13. *The spread of a massive drug culture*—which dominates the impoverished racial slums, in part as a form of psychological escape and in part as an alternative way to become rich quickly, with earnings from drugs estimated to yield more than $100 billion a year, and which is widespread also outside of such slums, particularly in the large urban centers;

14. *The inbreeding of social hopelessness*—which is becoming the normal outlook not only of the currently poor as well as of the homeless and especially of many young urban blacks, but includes also the several million who are already second- or even third-generation "addicts" to social welfare;

15. *The profusion of sexual license*—which, by becoming the dominant life-style, threatens the centrality of the family through the growing prevalence of the so-called one-parent family, in turn contributing to a dramatic loosening of primary bonds of social cohesion, not to speak of AIDS as one of its tragic side effects;

16. *The massive propagation of moral corruption by the visual media*—which under the guise of entertainment is engaged in the de facto advocacy of sex and violence as the means for attracting viewership and which in effect propagates instant self-gratification;

17. *A decline in civic consciousness*—which no longer demands

of the citizen any form of service or sacrifice on behalf of the nation-state;

18. *The emergence of potentially divisive multiculturalism*—which on the one hand represents an unavoidable recognition of the reality of the American mosaic but on the other threatens to balkanize multiethnic America by the deliberate deemphasis of the nationally unifying and socially equalizing effects of a common language and of shared historical traditions and political values;

19. *The emerging gridlock in the political system*—which has the effect of making the electorate feel that their government is remote, irresponsible, and corrupt, with special interests enjoying privileged access, and with the political elite enjoying unfair opportunities for indefinite self-perpetuation in office;

20. *An increasingly pervasive sense of spiritual emptiness*—which is felt by many who crave some transcendental belief but who find existing religious forms excessively ritualistic, unrelated to their dilemmas, with the churches also handicapped by their inability to compete for allegiance in the face of the cultural onslaught promoting licentious values.

Obviously, the above list could be much lengthened, or shortened, or qualified—depending on the perspective of the interpreter involved. Nonetheless, it can be postulated that the above summary encapsulates most of the basic dilemmas or shortcomings of contemporary America. At the same time, it must be hastily added that the above neither fully defines nor describes contemporary America. It is admittedly a caricature, though a caricature is meant to convey a quintessential truth. As such, it focuses deliberately on the factors needing redress if America is to remain globally vital and appealing.

The list contains within itself three broad and overlapping categories: the economic, the social, and even the metaphysical.

The first category pertains quite directly to America's capacity to compete with its economic rivals; the second involves the condition of the quality of life within American society; and the third bears on American values, expectations, and beliefs that cumulatively define America's character.

In the long run, it is the items in the second and third categories that are less likely to prove susceptible to decisive correction. Though the mainly economic agenda implied by the first category may appear to be overwhelming, it is in fact the kind of agenda that America is traditionally capable of tackling. It involves difficult, complex, and deeply ingrained problems—but still problems that Americans can identify and then attack. They are concrete, on the whole value free, and their resolution is likely to improve America's position vis-à-vis its economic rivals. This the American society can comprehend and this it can redress. In fact, to some extent, the counterattack is already in progress and is even beginning to make some headway.

In contrast, the broader social problems, and even more so the vaguer cultural ones, are not susceptible to quick responses. For one thing, the definition of the problem is more elusive. Hence the needed social consensus on a response is much more difficult to galvanize. For another, effective correction in some cases would require resolute political action, and that is more difficult in the complex and interlocking U.S. constitutional system. Moreover, social and especially cultural dilemmas are also ultimately philosophical in nature—and in most cases a response to them through governmental policy is not even pertinent.

Accordingly, it is likely that in the foreseeable future America will mount at least a partially effective response only to the first cluster of problems. There is growing evidence not only of widespread American recognition of the Japanese and European economic challenges but of a public determination in some fashion to respond. This is as true of the business community as it is of the political leadership. And even though a highly coordinated and massive national effort is unlikely to be undertaken, still on a number of fronts American performance is likely to improve.

The notion—so prevalent in the 1980s—that borrowing is the best way to avoid difficult socioeconomic dilemmas has already become discredited. The deficit—both budgetary and in trade—is recognized as a major challenge to the long-term economic health of the country. Similarly, one senses growing awareness that some deliberate initiatives designed to enhance U.S. industrial-technological competitiveness—even if not quite tantamount to a comprehensive "industrial policy"—will have to be undertaken. Studies by the Council on Competitiveness have identified areas of continued U.S. lead and of growing lag as the point of departure for an eventual counterattack.

It should also be noted that these studies confirm that the situation is not one-sidedly negative. While the American industries are weak or relatively noncompetitive in the broad areas of engineering and production, as well as electronic components, the American lead is still very strong in such broad categories as biotechnology, engines and propulsion, and information technologies. The American automobile industry is beginning to regain its competitive edge, with some U.S.-made models currently not only matching the Japanese ones in quality but actually more cost-effective in production. It is also noteworthy that in recent years new American companies have proven themselves to be more innovative and have grown more rapidly than comparable Japanese ones—thereby emphasizing the continuing capacity of the American economy for creative technological innovation and for successful industrial competition.

There is also developing consensus in both political parties regarding the need to upgrade the skills of American workers. Programs may vary—with some advocating apprentice programs and tax incentives for corporate-sponsored training, and with others advocating federally funded training programs as well as for-profit "proprietary" schools—but in any case it is evident that the problem is no longer being ignored. Moreover, though the overall increases in the productivity of American labor have lagged behind America's principal rivals during the last two decades, America's productivity in manufacturing (which still represents the most important sector of international trade) rose more rapidly during the decade of the 1980s than either Germany's or Japan's.

In addition, the first annual report to the president and Congress by the Competitiveness Policy Council (established by the Omnibus Trade and Competitiveness Act of 1988) has advocated a number of concrete measures designed to develop a national competitiveness strategy. The proposals for action focus on saving and investment, but they also advocate concrete remedies to such social weaknesses as education, training, and health care costs. Again, while it is unlikely that all will be implemented, the recommendations do reflect the growing public consciousness that purposeful action is urgently needed.

Finally, it is to be noted that at least to some degree the picture of an economically declining America is skewed by the unreliability of data. Many of the calculations which "prove" that the United States has already fallen behind its rivals in key indices of national wealth or general well-being are highly volatile, depending on the criteria that are used. For example, if market exchange rates are used, the United States ceases to be the per capita richest country, falling behind several European countries as well as Japan (despite the obvious limitations of the quality of life for the individual Japanese citizen). However, if purchasing power parity exchange rates are used, the United States remains number one, with Japan as far behind the United

States as the United States falls behind Japan when the earlier measuring yardstick is used.

The degree to which the United States lags behind Japan and Germany in actual investments in new technology, plants, and equipment is also highly dependent on the exchange rates that are used in the comparative calculations. Also, most comparisons ignore the fact that industrial construction in Japan tends to be infinitely more expensive than in the United States, which directly reduces the actual percentage of the Japanese investment dedicated to technological innovation. In brief, not only is the potential for American recovery often underestimated, but the picture of a technologically and industrially declining America, as contrasted with the dynamism of Japan or Western Europe, is also often overblown.

Unfortunately, more ominous for America's continued global preeminence are the implications of the social and philosophic dimensions of America's condition. These are no less important than the economic factors in determining America's likely global role. They influence the perception of America by the rest of the world, either thereby enhancing or constraining the role that America is able to play as the catalyst of global change.

In this connection, the biggest danger is posed by the collision between the intractability of America's social problems with the values that increasingly dominate America's culture and spirit. The former is the cumulative consequence of decades of discrimination, indifference, and lately, of paternalism. The results are huge islands of poverty, backwardness, and rejection, insulated from the rest of American life by invisible walls of prejudice and of a paternalism sufficiently concerned to prolong life but insufficiently caring to give it meaning. This condition is perpetuated by the gridlock of the American constitutional system, which inhibits concerted action to redeem—perhaps even through some form of compulsory training and employment—the millions that are thus threatened by permanent exclusion from participation in the hallowed (but, alas, also increasingly ritualistic) notion of America as a society of opportunity.

The reality must be faced that a major improvement in this regard is unlikely to be forthcoming without a significant shift in the predominant values of American society. With the fading of religion and of patriotism, the "Horatio Alger" philosophy has become the dominant ethic. Its downside is contempt for failure and the conviction that poverty is somehow self-inflicted. Persistent racism—which has not been eradicated from American society—reinforces the prevailing moral complacency regarding the underprivileged. Moreover, the current emphasis—especially by the dominant purveyors of mass culture—on the worship of material wealth, on consumption, and on the propagation of self-indulgence as the definition of the good life creates blinders to the key social dilemmas, inhibiting a response that could over time generate genuinely effective remedial action.

The particularly negative role in shaping American values played by television has already been noted earlier. It is this medium that has become predominant in shaping the national culture and its basic beliefs. As James B. Twitchell observes, in his incisive *Carnival Culture—The Trashing of Taste in America* (1992), American TV has become "a medium whose input is so profound and so resolutely banal that it has almost single-handedly removed vulgarity from modern culture by making it the norm." The result is a mass culture, driven by profiteers who exploit the hunger for vulgarity, pornography, and even barbarism. Such supremacy of decadence and hedonism in a culture cannot help but have a demoralizing effect on the values of society, undermining and eroding once more deeply felt beliefs.

TV has had a particularly important effect in disrupting generational continuity in the transfer of traditions and values. TV entertainment—and even news—have gone overboard in sensa-tionalizing reality as novelty detached from any moral moorings and in presenting material or sexual self-gratification as the normal, even admirable, conduct. It is striking to observe the degree to which the most popular programs designed for young audiences—as well as the most widely viewed "talk" shows—concentrate on decadence and debauchery while applauding the rejection of traditional authority. In words that some might as-cribe to a fundamentalist preacher but in fact appeared in a survey in *The Economist* (March 28, 1992), the most-viewed American TV programs for teenagers presented their parents typically "as emotionally erratic, divorced, white-collar crimi-nals, hooked on alcohol or cocaine or New Age crystals." This hardly enhances parental ability to transmit values to children.

The marked decline of the nuclear family as the basic social unit aggravates the cultural-philosophical malaise of contempo-rary America. That decline is the direct product of changing social values, as reflected in and propagated by the mass media. Family implies structure, responsibility, and restraint. The very requirements of good family life work against the grain of unin-hibited hedonism, for they impose the obligations of sacrifice, loyalty, and trust. In contrast, the weakening of family ties makes the individual more susceptible to fads, fashions, and thus also to an increasingly fluid inner faith which, before long, becomes transformed into a self-serving justification for egocentrism. All of this is inimical to the generation of enduring principles, not to speak of some socially shared criteria of self-denial.

America clearly needs a period of philosophical introspection and of cultural self-critique. It must come to grips with the realization that a relativist hedonism as the basic guide to life offers no firm social moorings, that a community which partakes of no shared absolute certainties but which instead puts a premium on individual self-satisfaction is a community threatened by dissolution. However, any attempt at American retrospection and renewal will have to be pursued in a much more complex setting than in the past. The ethnic and cultural composition of America is changing profoundly. By the year 2010, one out of every five Americans is likely to be of Hispanic origin, one of African or Asian origin, and three of European. By 2050 the ratios are likely to be two, one, and two, respectively. In other words, the European component will drop from 60 percent to about 40 percent. This will be a very different America from the largely European America of the recent past, one more likely to mirror the cultural and philosophical cleavages that already divide the world.

The transformation of America from a society dominated—and shaped—by a white Anglo-Saxon Protestant culture into a global mosaic inevitably will involve a profound shift in values and perhaps some further loss of social cohesion. While such a change may generate new creativity and dynamism—and its intellectual and human benefits are undeniable—it is also likely to be disruptive, even potentially divisive, especially if in the process the unifying function of a common language and of an inculcated common political philosophy are deliberately downgraded. A shared language and a shared constitutional commitment produce the common foundation on which a nation's cultural consensus rests, and without them cultural diversity could become incapable of sustaining social tolerance. The American society could then face the threat of disintegration.

It is easy to label such a concern as racist but to do so is to evade—and even to precipitate—the resulting problems. One simply cannot ignore the high probability that the recreation of the global cultural and ethnic mosaic within a very differentiated America will actually make it more difficult to address the social and cultural dilemmas that the country confronts. Indeed, in the absence of major progress in dealing compassionately with these dilemmas, the new mosaic could generate within America even escalating urban guerrilla warfare. To say this is not tantamount to the rejection of the change in the ethnic makeup of America that in any case is almost inevitable, but it is to suggest that the needed cultural renewal is more likely to be forthcoming if the essential linguistic and philosophical sources of national unity are deliberately preserved.

The danger to American global preeminence generated by America's internal social and cultural dilemmas is thus twofold: on the one hand, the image of a society guided largely by cornucopian aspirations devoid of deeper human values tends to undermine the global appeal of the American social model, especially as the symbol of freedom; on the other hand, that image tends to generate highly exaggerated material expectations among the vast masses of the world's poorer majority, expectations which cannot conceivably be satisfied yet the frustration of which is bound to intensify their resentment of global inequality.

THREE

The Faceless Rivals

If America were to falter—unable to project effective global authority—are there rivals with the capacity to replace (or displace) America? What currently existing state has the potential—and especially the political will to greatness—to match America in the four critical components of global power? Which can project a compelling message and back it up with muscular national assertiveness?

Without an instinctive, organic national aspiration (which need not even be forcefully articulated) nations do not emerge as great powers. Only those which in some indefinable manner produce a culturally spontaneous outburst of assertive, competitive, and driving desire to explore and to conquer transform themselves into an entity that becomes demonstrably more dominant than others. That desire reflects a mysterious sense of mission expressed through wholehearted dedication of countless individuals who partake of a shared commitment to the glory and destiny of national greatness.

At different stages of history, that special desire, which successfully fuses the initiative of individuals with the collective weal, transformed the city of Rome into a European and Mediterranean empire, the island of England into a maritime global empire, and the Duchy of Muscovy into a continental empire. And much the same was the case with Spain, France, and even post–World War II America. No single individual willed that it should be so, but countless individuals spontaneously partook of a historical aspiration and were committed to its attainment.

But will alone—individual and collective—will not suffice. The emergence of great powers is also the consequence of special historical opportunity combined with inherent physical capability. The moment—or the historical trend—must be congenial to the flowering of a dominant, catalytic state that has something of importance to say to the world at large—be it through a *mission civilisatrice* or a doctrinal revelation or a compelling social example—to which others are historically receptive. Last but not least, extant must be the necessary sinews of power, economic and also military.

In the foreseeable future, does the above apply to, and fit the likely circumstances of, Japan and Europe respectively? At this stage of history, only these two—especially because of their economic power—loom as the most likely pretenders to America's mantle. It has become fashionable, therefore, to project the emergence of these two as the successors to America's superpower status. Since their respective situations and prospects differ, each must be assessed separately.

National will plays a special role in the case of Japan. Less than half a century ago, in the late spring of 1945, Japan was literally burning. Its driving ambition to claim a share in global power as Asia's preeminent state—the sponsor and organizer of the "Asian coprosperity sphere"—was turning to ashes. Fifty years of sustained effort, initiated by Japan's spectacular victory over Russia, and which culminated in a massive war simultaneously against China and America, were drawing to a bitter end—

to a humiliating and crushing defeat. If there was ever a moment for soul searching, for despair, and certainly for a scaling down of national ambitions, this was it.

On April 11, 1945, a professor at Tokyo University was visited by a friend, a youngish official from "the Ministry of Greater East Asia." The two had a long and private talk about Japan's war and postwar prospects. The official was a thoughtful economist, with a penchant for longer-range planning. The two concluded that the war was lost. But that did not mean that everything else was lost. According to the visitor, Japan should now draw a central lesson from its tragic experience, namely "that Japan, poorly endowed with natural resources, must shape its future around developing precision engineering." The professor, with evident enthusiasm, in his diary cites his visitor as drawing a historical metaphor in support of his principal message:

> A poor warrior wanted to buy a splendid suit of armor but had no money, so he cut down on the amount of food he ate and little by little saved enough to buy a fine suit of armor. A war broke out and courageously he left to fight, but because his body had become so weak from his years of semistarvation, he could not bear the weight of his armor and was soon slain by the enemy.
>
> This was just what happened to Japan. He did not think that a defeated Japan would be allowed to rearm at all, but this would probably be a blessing in disguise. Japan did not have the qualities of a first-class power, but she could excel as a second-class power.
>
> I completely agreed with all he said. I will actually be happy if rearmament is completely prohibited. An army in uniform is not the only sort of army. Scientific technology and fighting spirit under a business suit will be our underground army. This Japanese-American war can be taken as the khaki losing to the

business suits. Today I am in unusually high spirits because I have found a sympathetic ear.

The entire passage appears in the autobiography *Japan's Challenging Years: Reflections on my Lifetime*, by the distinguished Japanese economic planner and, in the late 1970s, one-time foreign minister, Saburo Okita, an individual who has come to personalize Japan's positive involvement in world affairs. In his account, Okita went on to describe how he and some associates, abjuring despair, immediately set to work—despite the ongoing war—to plan for Japan's postwar recovery and for its new international role. Japan's indomitable spirit was to infuse that role with a driving competitive zeal, bearing in mind the injunction already quoted: "An army in uniform is not the only sort of army. Scientific technology and fighting spirit under a business suit will be our underground army."

This was back in 1945. Half a century later, many already feel that America in "the khaki [is] losing to the business suits" worn by the Japanese. Undeniably, there is ample evidence that the Japanese recovery has been motivated by single-mindedness, well expressed in the remarkably revealing and historically important passages cited above. The Japanese national sense of unique identity, the cohesion of its national community, the special ability of its society to generate a shared sense of direction, and the persistent pursuit of longer-range strategic goals have cumulatively propelled Japan again to the front ranks of world economic power.

That power, in the years immediately ahead, will continue to grow. Even if the momentum of Japan's economic growth were to slow down, in the course of the next two decades Japan will, at the very least, consolidate its already remarkable position as the world's number two national economy, and it may come

close to matching or—depending also on America's performance—even surpassing the United States as the source of the
world's largest GNP. Data in support of this prognosis are so
abundant that the matter is not even in dispute. Indeed, the only
uncertainty pertains to the extent to which Japan's growth might
contribute to the undermining of key American industrial sectors
and to the degree to which the United States could be outpaced
as the technological/scientific leader of the global economy.
Related to this uncertainty is the matter of America's financial
vulnerability to Japan's leverage, given the persisting American
deficits and massive trade imbalances in American-Japanese
trade.

Concerns regarding these issues have generated in the United
States a veritable cottage industry of ominous predictions, ranging from speculations about America's displacement by Japan as
the world's superpower to best-selling novels about a renewed
American-Japanese military collision. At the very least, the expectation that Japan will soon become a comprehensive global
power has become deeply embedded in American—and also in
European—thinking about the world of the future.

There is no doubt that much can be cited in support of
that view. Massive literature—much of it alarmist—is available,
prognosticating Japan's inevitable rise to a dominant global position. The case is generally derived from the special qualities
and motivation of the Japanese society as well as the related
momentum of Japanese economic growth. It is, on the whole, a
compelling case. Social values, it is said, give Japan a special
competitive advantage over America, especially since Japanese
social priorities involve dedication first to one's company, then
to one's country, then to one's family, and finally to oneself. In
contrast, American social values are the exact opposite. Japanese
priorities help to create a community that partakes spontaneously
of a shared goal—the equivalent of the will to greatness—that

can then be channeled intelligently by an elite that deliberately looks and plans far ahead.

Japan's recovery and rise to global financial-economic preeminence has certainly been facilitated by these special characteristics, enabling the country to set for itself—decade by decade—special targets, to concentrate its resources, to engage in sustained R & D, and then to exploit its comparative advantage. Moreover, the relatively small defense burden and social frugality have enabled the Japanese to sustain a rate of domestic savings, relative to the GNP, that in recent years has been well in excess of twice that of America's. Saving, planning, and investing—areas where America has been particularly lax—have been the not-so-secret real reasons for Japan's economic success—and not the wildly exaggerated American charges that Japan has discriminated against American exports. (Some calculations have suggested that the U.S. trade deficit with Japan would shrink by only about 20 percent even if Japan were to satisfy every American demand regarding trade access.)

While any specific figures are of doubtful accuracy—given the complications of comparative purchasing power parities—it is nonetheless clear that with a considerably smaller GNP than America's, Japan still has been able to undertake industrial R & D that already comes close to matching America's. By 1991, the Japanese were dominating even U.S. patent awards, with four Japanese corporations leading the way, and with an American corporation only in fifth place. A survey conducted in the same year by the Japanese Economic Planning Agency concluded that whereas American firms still dominated critical technologies in forty-three areas, Japanese firms were not far behind, leading in thirty-three. And if the Japanese economy continues to grow at annual rates roughly twice that of America, and if the yen were to appreciate close to 100-to-1 relative to the dollar (both "ifs" being admittedly major but not altogether unrealistic assumptions), it is possible that within a decade or so Japan's GNP could begin to match America's.

The attainment of economic preeminence (thanks to the combination of "scientific technology and fighting spirit") is likely to further fuel the Japanese national pride and perhaps expand Japanese political ambitions. Japanese nationalism is clearly already on the rise. Japanese martial virtues have again become very popular subjects of literature and of the mass media. Even the highly internationalist former prime minister Yasuhiro Nakasone has spoken proudly of Japan's racial homogeneity (contrasting its allegedly consequent higher intelligence with the racially and ethnically American heterogeneity) and has extolled the virtues of the "Yamato" tradition, with its assertions of universal superiority. The fervor with which the spokesmen for Japanese national greatness—ranging from the outspoken politician Shintaro Ishihara to the internationalist business leader Akio Morita—speak of Japan's special role, and the increasingly open manifestations of contempt for America, could foreshadow a bid for global political leadership, with economic prowess as its launchpad.

That bid could be hastened by friction with the United States. Each society tends to view the other through skewed mirrors and distorted lenses. Many Japanese see Americans increasingly as living in a declining state. They gloat over real or imagined American deficiencies, lap up every book or article—usually produced by the Americans themselves—that presents America as sliding down history's drain. At the same time, Americans concentrate on a vision of Japan as a society driven by totally selfish economic motives, unfairly exploiting American military protection to dump its industrial-technological products on America while driving Americans out of their jobs.

In their turn, American public attacks on Japanese business and trade practices, though often justified on their merits, have further intensified anti-American Japanese resentments, fueled by the suspicion that the American preoccupation with Japan as an economic threat has an underlying racial motivation. That tends to infuse into Japanese nationalism an emotional motivation that could be channeled into political and chauvinist directions, as already some Japanese politicians have been tempted to do.

Their task may be made easier by the inadvertent consequences of U.S. policies, especially in the area of American-Japanese security relations. Viewed in a historical perspective, the long-standing U.S. policy to encourage Japan to assume a more active international role in the area of military security and to spend more on armaments is questionable from the standpoint of regional stability and the American national interest. Admittedly, on narrow geopolitical grounds, the case for pressing Japan to assume a higher military profile has some superficial legitimacy. It is odd—by traditional international standards—for a country of some 120 million people, with the second largest GNP in the world, to be almost defenseless in the face of powerful neighbors and to be so dependent on the military protection of a distant ally that is also a former enemy and a current economic rival.

Some enhancement in Japan's regional military capability seems, therefore, justified and desirable. It would reduce American burdens and make Japan more self-sufficient and more self-reliant. Moreover, in an unstable world which for its security requires enhanced international cooperation, Japan's abstinence from participation in international peacekeeping can be viewed as an act of delinquency. That, in any case, has been the American argument, and sustained pressure has been brought to bear on Tokyo to encourage Japan to assume larger international security responsibilities. American military planners have also been prompting the Japanese to widen the perimeter of Japan's maritime and air responsibilities for Far Eastern security.

However, one has to wonder whether it has been historically wise for the United States to encourage and even to pressure Japan to plunge into a truly more active military role. Such external American prompting has been contributing to the progressive breakdown of Japanese inhibitions against the assumption of the more traditional trappings of world power. These inhibitions—while not negating Japanese national ambitions regarding global status (which have remained remarkably strong, despite Japan's defeat in World War II)—have at least had the beneficial effect of steering Japan's global involvement into more benign "civilian" directions.

It would be a supreme historical irony if shortsighted American policy were to provide the justification, as well as the impetus, for the revival of Japan's more traditional imperial yearnings. This could prompt, over time, both a massive buildup of Japan's own arms industry and a gradual disconnection between the American and Japanese security interests. It is noteworthy that the very public American pressure on Japan to become more actively involved in the Gulf War effort of 1991 led one prominent Japanese businessman to propose (in *Yomiuri Shimbun* of May 20, 1991) that U.S. forces should leave Japan, that the Japanese-American security treaty be revised, and that "Tokyo should also cooperate with Seoul and Beijing to create an Asian security system independent of the superpowers."

It is, therefore, timely to ponder the question: can an ambitiously aroused Japan effectively challenge America's comprehensive global preeminence if Japan confines itself to remaining primarily an economic superpower; and can Japan become a comprehensive global superpower itself, especially if encouraged by America to seek the more traditional political and military attributes of superpower status?

A detached judgment, not fueled by irritations generated by ongoing trade frictions (not to speak of irrational anti-Japanese emotions), yields skeptical conclusions. First of all, Japan's global economic leadership is not foreordained, because very much depends on the competitive response of America (which, as noted earlier, is already developing). Moreover, Japan's dependence on foreign trade, raw materials, and its aging population do suggest certain major limits to any exponential projections of Japan's growth. Demographic dynamics pose a particularly serious threat to Japan's longer-range prospects. It has been estimated that by the year 2010 a considerably higher percentage of Japan's population than America's will fall into the relatively unproductive age bracket of sixty-five or more—thereby dramatically reducing the likely Japanese rates of savings and investment.

Moreover, Japanese economic priorities are gradually beginning to shift. The new five-year plan adopted in mid-1992 by the Economic Planning Agency urged Japan to try to become a leader in preserving the global environment and to boost its own standard of living by increasing domestic consumption instead of concentrating on production for foreign exports. It is likely that over time such shifts in overall priorities will begin to have an impact not only on Japanese life-styles but will alter both the rate and the content of Japanese economic growth.

In addition, economic power by itself does not translate into political power. This is especially the case with an economic superpower that conveys no social or philosophical vision to the world, and that is also extraordinarily vulnerable to any international conflicts or even disruptions. A good example of the inherent limits to any potential Japanese aspirations to become the global superpower is provided by the Japanese experience with foreign aid. Japan is today the world's most generous donor of Overseas Development Aid, exceeding by far America's contributions. Yet relatively little political credit accrues to Japan because of its generosity. This is so because most recipients view

that aid as some form of tax—or entitlement—obtained in return
for Japan's exploitation of their natural resources and access to
their markets. The political benefits for Japan involve at most
merely a reduction in anti-Japanese hostility, but without a significant improvement in the widespread perception of Japan as
a selfish nation.

This reluctance to credit Japan's good deeds is largely the
result of the fact that Japan impacts on but does not speak to the
world. As a society, it offers the world neither an appealing social
model nor a relevant message. Its cultural homogeneity makes
Japan—quite unlike America—into a less congenial participant
in the increasingly open and organic global political process.
America is the world in a microcosm; insular Japan is unlike
the rest of the world. That makes American leadership seem
somewhat more natural and thus more acceptable. In contrast,
any attempt at the assertion of Japanese global leadership would
be instinctively resisted as remote and organically alien.

Furthermore, Japan's compressed and crowded cities do not
create the image of a life-style that others yearn to imitate and
enjoy. Its language—difficult and spoken by no one else—reinforces a sense of exclusiveness and distance. Its politics—a
translated adaptation to Japanese culture of American democracy—have become corrupt and secretive, with traditional loyalties and personal political fiefdoms becoming at least as
important as formal constitutional structures. As one Japanese
politician put it, "Our country has a first-rate economy, second-
rate standard of living, and third-rate political system"—a combination not likely to help translate global economic power, and
even nascent military power, into effective global authority.

Last but not least, Japan's economic prowess is made possible
by global conditions that are relatively stable and secure. To the
extent that such stability and security are dependent on the
decisions—and goodwill—of another power, Japan must defer

to it, unless it is prepared to risk calamity. As Japan's wealth increases, its dependence on such global stability will grow further. Present indications suggest, for instance, that the production and export of Asian crude oil will be unable to keep up with Japan's growing demand. Thus Japan's dependence on imports from the Persian Gulf—a region dominated largely by the United States—will greatly increase in the course of this decade, and so will Japan's precarious dependence on stable and normal international conditions.

Most of Japan's current political and business elite is historically quite sober and knows that Japan cannot hope to free itself from external dependence by the development of major military capabilities. On the whole, the Japanese have prudently resisted America's misguided encouragement of an enhanced Japanese military role. But even if that reluctance were to recede and Japan were to undertake a politically significant expansion of its military capabilities, based on its impressive GNP and especially on its technological skills, it does not follow that Japan would gain thereby enhanced global political clout. Indeed, the consequences for Japan could be even quite negative.

There is a compelling reason for this. Unlike Europe, where Germany's rearmament has been subsumed within NATO (with the German army not having even its own general staff) and offset also by European economic and growing political integration, a militarily powerful Japan would be on its own in Asia. That would automatically evoke historically motivated fear and loathing. It could place in jeopardy Japanese foreign investments and undermine Japanese trade. It could galvanize anti-Japanese coalitions and almost certainly precipitate intense antagonism on the part of both Korea and China—and eventually even America, despite the American role in undermining initial Japanese inhibitions against rearmament.

A militarily powerful Japan would quickly become an isolated

Japan. In itself, that would make it impossible to translate Japanese power into Japanese leadership. American military power—indeed, even military presence abroad—was at one point fervently desired by the Europeans, the Koreans, and also by the Japanese themselves. Yet it is difficult to conceive of a country, in Asia or elsewhere, that would welcome the emergence of solitary Japanese military might. The brutal reality is that through militarization Japan could become only a disruptive superpower rather than a constructive one.

In turn, by standing armed but alone, Japan would make itself vulnerable to the progressive destruction of its underlying economic strength, which is derived from, and dependent upon, continued and growing international cooperation. In effect, reaching out for truly comprehensive military power (beyond merely some marginal enhancement of Japan's already quite impressive but still essentially defensive forces) would be tantamount to undermining the comprehensive economic underpinnings of such potential global political power. It would be a suicidal policy even in the economic domain.

It is noteworthy that astute Chinese observers, who closely monitor Japan's growing power, have concluded that ultimately a break in the American-Japanese connection is unlikely. This is a matter of obvious importance to Chinese policy planners, and their assessment deserves note. While the Chinese strategic analysts do expect that economic frictions between Japan, the United States, and the European Community will grow, their conclusion has been (according to the report of the Beijing Institute for International Strategic Studies, no. 1, March 1991) that "the United States and Japan will not become foes" because of the inherent limitations on Japanese power of the growing American-Japanese interdependence and of the growth of international economic cooperation.

Realistic Japanese leaders recognize these limitations. Increasingly, they call upon Japan to become more conscious of the obligation to pursue macroeconomic policies that will mitigate Japan's structural underconsumption and thus somewhat reduce current account surpluses. They also call upon Japan to define for itself a novel and truly constructive global role, especially in the area of development. They recognize Japan's stake in a vital—and not weak and resentful—America. They accordingly define Japan's goals in a more subdued fashion, emphasizing Japan's role as a new "civilian" power, closely related to America and aspiring to play, in effect, the role of a global "vice president" (as one Japanese leader put it). Closeness to America, perhaps even some sort of an ambiguous global partnership with America—but not a head-on challenge to America's leadership—is accepted by them as the best guarantee of Japan's growing global status.

That partnership will doubtless be confronted by continuing internal frictions, but, most probably, it will also continue to take shape. The reality of economic interdependence between America and Japan is beginning to permeate the thinking of the political elites and the practices of the economic elites of the two countries. Indeed, eventual Japanese accession to the North American Free Trade Area is more likely than a head-on American-Japanese collision. Eventually, a trans-Pacific American-Japanese cooperative community (I have called it elsewhere "Amerippon") might even emerge. Inherent in that process is the tacit recognition that an outright Japanese challenge to America's global leadership would be more likely to burst the Japanese bubble than to prompt the replacement of America by Japan.

What then of Europe? Europe, as the alternative contender for global leadership, is strong where Japan is weak. Therefore, it might be in a better position to exploit its economic potential in order to project a globally compelling social message and to seek global military power. It has the cultural and linguistic capacity to make itself a highly relevant, but also catalytic, participant in the increasingly organic global political process. It already possesses, on a national basis, significant military power. Moreover, the attainment of a common military organization would not precipitate for Europe the adverse political and economic consequences inherent in any Japanese effort to acquire a major military capability.

Moreover, like Japan, Europe has the potential capacity to match and outstrip the United States in economic-financial power, as it has already done in the volume of world trade. European rates of savings, like the Japanese, are considerably higher than America's. European technology is certainly also competitive. The Japanese survey mentioned earlier concluded that European firms were leading in 34 of the 110 critical technologies assessed. Europe is, however, less dependent than Japan on the outside world—possessing a larger territory, generating more internal trade, and enjoying more secure access to natural resources. Finally, as in the case of Japan, Europe partakes of a history that predisposes it to define for itself a sense of mission, and therefore it has the will to greatness.

The message that Europe could aspire to convey to the world—depending, of course, on Europe's further development and unification—could be an extrapolation of the best of the American way of life without the worst. The standard of living in the northwestern portions of Europe is at least comparable to America's and is not blighted by urban decay. Even its current racial and ethnic dilemmas are not on the scale of America's. Urban slums in this part of Europe are practically nonexistent and, for example, only 5 percent of German children live in poverty, while in America more than 22 percent do.

Moreover, Western Europe has made considerable progress in the development of a social policy that does not stifle creative private enterprise and yet assures the individual more than the minimum requisites for a relatively secure standard of living. At least in Germany, Scandinavia, Benelux, and France, health care, maternity benefits, social pensions, paid vacations, unemployment compensation—in addition to effective primary and secondary educational systems—more than match the American model. Last but not least, the level of crime and the scope of the drug epidemic are lower.

The foregoing provides the foundation for making the case that in the foreseeable future Europe could become the catalytic "state" of the global community. Indeed, its rich philosophic and artistic traditions perhaps could help to infuse into American mass culture—to which the European youth has become very susceptible—greater intellectual content, thereby somewhat tempering its crass and vulgar edges. Also to much of the world, the European centers of learning—notably in Great Britain and in France—still exercise considerable attraction, even though American graduate schools are now considered to be globally preeminent.

The cultural heterogeneity of Europe is a further asset. Much of the world has been influenced by, and remains still within reach of, the French, English, Spanish, Portuguese, or German languages. To the extent that Europe, as it unites, becomes probably trilingual, it will be in a position to challenge America's dominant role in the ongoing global chatter and certainly will not have the difficulties Japan faces in participating actively in the global political or intellectual dialogue.

Though the hold of religion on European culture has greatly waned, and Europe today—even more so than America—is essentially a secular society, the impact of the common Christian tradition still lingers. It gives Europe the underpinnings of a shared ethical system and simultaneously infuses European culture with a universal philosophical relevance. The location of the

Catholic church's Holy See reinforces that condition, creating a special bond with the hundreds of millions of Christians in Latin America, Africa, and Asia. Unlike Japan, Europe in its very body and soul has been universalist rather than exclusivistic.

European nations also have had a deeply ingrained will to greatness. Historically, this expressed itself in the dynamic outreach of its explorers and then empire builders, and more tragically in the European fratricide that ultimately led in the twentieth century to Europe's political suicide. In recent history, the will to greatness has assumed a European identity, embodied most ambitiously by France and Germany respectively. Charles de Gaulle, perhaps the most eloquent articulator of national grandeur, was seized with the idea that true greatness in this historical epoch could only be achieved through a common European effort and in a common European home stretching to the Urals—even if still led by France.

Much of the impetus for Europe's unification has been derived from a more widely shared sentiment rooted in that common aspiration. There is an awareness that a united Europe would not only put behind itself mutually destructive national conflicts but would also automatically become a preeminent world-class superpower. To many Germans, Britons, and Frenchmen—especially among the political elites—that vision still exercises a powerful attraction, derived from deeply internalized national ambitions. History of past greatness, and even of unfulfilled national aspirations, is a significant source of the motivation to build a single and eventually powerful Europe.

A politically united Europe would have to have military power. Notwithstanding American objections to the emergence of a European military component outside NATO, the political unification of Europe would almost inevitably push Europe toward some integration of its armed forces. The Franco-German corps in all probability would serve as its nucleus, while the Franco-British nuclear forces already give Europe a respectable nuclear deterrent. The projected and very significant cuts in U.S. and Russian nuclear delivery systems and warheads, agreed to in 1992 and to be implemented by the next decade, will further enhance the relative strategic significance of Europe's military power.

Unlike the case of Japan, that potential development does not threaten Europe either with political isolation or with negative economic consequences. Quite the contrary. Many see in the unification of Europe and in the development by Europe of a common defense force the best guarantee against any resumption of traditional European conflicts. In such a wider continental context Germany's power will be sublimated, thus finally resolving the challenge to Europe's balance of power posed during this century by the emergence of Germany as Europe's single most powerful national state. Accordingly, a militarily self-reliant Europe would be perceived as reinforcing global stability, rather than threatening it.

Finally, Europe has clearly the capacity to match and to surpass even America's economic power. With a considerably larger and well-educated population, with an internal market larger than America's, with a global trade also bigger than the American, and with a combined GNP that already outstrips America's, a united Europe would automatically be more than a peer of the United States and of Japan. It would also be a hard-driving competitor. European reactions to the Japanese economic challenge—while less politically strident than the American—have already demonstrated not only Europe's determination to compete but also its willingness to play hardball regarding discriminatory practices. Whether as "a fortress Europe"—limiting global free trade—or, more likely, as a relatively open but highly competitive single market, Europe's economic potential could serve as the basis for reaching out also for military power, for cultural impact, and thus also for global political clout.

This potential has already led to some remarkable changes in the European perspective on its relationship with America. The quintessence of that change is conveyed by the substance of two European best-sellers, which appeared a decade and a half apart. The first, by Jean-Jacques Servan-Schreiber and originally entitled *Le Défi Américain* (1975) postulated a world dominated by America, with Europe very much in a secondary position, incapable of competing or coping with the spreading control by American corporations of the global markets. The second, much more recent, by Jacques Attali, entitled *Lignes d'Horizon* (1991), conveys a dramatically different message: celebrating America's alleged decline, it predicts a Europe that outstrips both America and Japan as the global nerve center and catalyst.

How correct is this more recent, and equally extreme, prognosis? How likely is it in fact that Europe will emerge as the successful contender for America's mantle? The entire case made in the foregoing pages rests or falls on one basic and critically important—yet very uncertain—assumption: that Europe will go beyond economic unity to political unity and in the process acquire also significant military strength. Accordingly, the argument made thus far is essentially for the proposition that Europe has a far greater *potential* for emerging as America's rival than does Japan—*but that is not the same as saying that Europe will actually do so.*

In fact, Europe is unlikely to attain, in the near future, genuine political unity and hence acquire a defined military identity. Though the process of unification is not likely to be halted completely—and, almost certainly, it is even less likely to be reversed—the most probable trend is that of a continued but very difficult integration, with phases of progress punctuated by occasional major setbacks. That, cumulatively, makes it unlikely that Europe in the foreseeable future could emerge as a politically united challenger to America's special global status. Eventually it might, but certainly not soon.

There are several reasons for such a firm prognosis. The first pertains to the various internal and external obstacles that impede genuine political unification; the second pertains to the security implications of the increased difficulty of defining Europe's actual scope; and the third to the negative effect of some domestic trends within the core European nations on Europe's global message.

Although Europe is committed to the goal of unity, both the substantive definition and the geographic scope of that unity remain a bone of contention. The European Community committed itself at the Maastricht Summit of 1992 to become the European Union, both economically and politically, within this decade; to have a single currency by 1997 (by 1999 at the latest); and to become a single market by 1993. All of this, however, entails a process in which complex financial and economic, as well as political, issues are to be progressively resolved, on the basis of the continued and explicit support of the various European electorates. In essence, it involves a step-by-step overcoming of obstacles through complex negotiations, which are then subject to national political approval.

There is no other approach, given the existing political and institutional realities of the recovered Europe. A leap into unity might have been possible earlier, by a Europe devastated by two wars and dependent on American decision making. That is no longer an option. But a complex process inherently means that basic strategic disagreements are bound to surface repeatedly, periodically reopening even previously resolved issues. A negative reaction by the electorate of one European country is likely to be followed by a positive reaction by another, and then again by a negative one, etc. It is, therefore, not surprising that the timetable set in Maastricht has slipped.

As a result, the question of how deep Europe's integration is to become will periodically collide with the historically timely question of how wide Europe's unity is to become. The collapse of the Soviet bloc has placed that issue on Europe's agenda. It can no longer be evaded, not only in regard to the EFTA (European Free Trade Area) countries but also in regard to the post-communist triangle of Poland, Hungary, and Czechoslovakia (or the latter's two successor states). These Central European countries will press hard for membership, seeing in it the salvation for their domestic woes.

The result is a collision between two broad concepts of Europe early in the next century: the first entails the economically integrated European Community soon becoming the European Union, with some enlargement in regard to the EFTA countries and in this decade with no more than associate status for the Central European triangle; the second envisages a much larger Europe, embracing even within this decade both the EFTA and the Central European countries. The former is likely to be politically more cohesive and more apt then to reach out for a genuine military component (based on the Franco-German Corps); the latter inevitably would involve some dilution of political cohesion (which is why the British so strongly favor it).

Within the former, Germany is more likely to be firmly anchored; within the latter, Germany is more likely to be freer to flirt with its own national policy, perhaps as America's principal continental partner but perhaps not excluding the eventual possibility of some sort of a German-Russian accommodation. Within the former, political leadership is more likely to be exercised by a continuing Franco-German partnership; within the latter, both the United Kingdom and the United States may be in a better position to exercise subtle influence.

These dilemmas are going to keep resurfacing, promoting periodic clashes among the key European players. Moreover, even if the process of deepening were to continue in a straight line, the need for widening cannot be entirely ignored. The nonmembers will pound at the doors of the European Community—and their exclusion could be politically unsettling, especially in Central Europe. Hence ultimately some combination of deepening and of widening is likely to be inevitable, thereby automatically complicating the quest for political unity.

That quest, in any case, still has to overcome the residual resistance of separate European national identities and of specific national interests. France appears to be willing to become truly part of a larger Europe, thereby even subordinating its national sovereignty on key political issues to a new European authority, but only if France then leads (with German acquiescence and partnership) the politically united Europe. Germany is prepared to propitiate European fears of its power by becoming truly integrated into Europe, providing other European countries also are fully integrated and provided that on economic-financial matters the German lead is de facto accepted. Britain is prepared to be part of a more united Europe, provided that Europe is not so united as to exclude room for traditional British maneuvering, enhanced by a continued American influence in Europe (with the latter reinforced by the special Anglo-American relationship).

These specific national interests are not inherently incompatible. However, they not only complicate but also unavoidably delay the process of unification. To truly unify, Europe must either fashion a remarkable degree of consensus—or be led by an acknowledged leader, guided by a clear and compelling historical vision. Given Europe's deeply embedded national diversity, the first will inevitably take years while the second, under the current circumstances, is impossible to impose.

Of the European states, France has come the closest to articulating a politically ambitious vision of Europe's future. De Gaulle particularly spoke in terms that captivated the hearts and minds of many Europeans, as on Dec. 31, 1963:

> Without ceding to the illusions in which the weak indulge, but without losing the hope that men's freedom and dignity will everywhere win the day, we must envisage a time when, perhaps, in Warsaw, Prague, Budapest, Bucharest, Sofia, Belgrade, Tirana and Moscow, the communist totalitarian regime, which still manages to imprison peoples, might gradually come to a development reconcilable with our own transformation. Then, prospects matching her resources and capacities would be open to the whole of Europe.

Yet France remains too weak—especially after the reunification of Germany—to impose its leadership on other Europeans. Moreover, the others—even the Germans—are not prepared to accept the French definition of European political identity as entailing Europe's self-assertion against America. On the contrary, most Europeans believe that a close and continued association with the United States, especially in the security area, is still in Europe's basic interest. This inherently limits the acceptability of a leadership that places a premium on European self-assertion.

The quest for Europe's unity, moreover, is now burdened by a historically new—though welcome—question, one which Europe can no longer ignore: where does Europe end? Until recently, to speak of Europe meant to speak of Western Europe. The rest was east of the Iron Curtain. Today, there are basically three Europes: "Europe 1"—the unifying Western Europe; "Europe 2"—the Central Europeans, who insist that culturally they partake of the same traditions as the West Europeans and who are anxious to become united with Europe as soon as possible; and "Europe 3"—the East Europeans of the former Soviet

Union, some of whom hope eventually to become part of Europe while fearing the consequences of prolonged exclusion.

Just a few numbers convey the scale of the problem: the currently existing European Community is made up of twelve states containing 343 million people. Before too long, the five EFTA countries are likely to be associated, increasing the total population of integrating Europe—of "Europe 1"—to about 370 million people. But pounding at the doors of "Europe 1" are the Europeans of "Europe 2"—of Poland, Hungary, Czechoslovakia, and Slovenia—with an additional 70 million people. Their eventual entry would increase Europe (counting also natural growth) to about 450 million people and twenty-seven states—a massive and complex organism, not susceptible to prompt political integration.

Although the more immediate problem facing the architects of Europe is to define some sort of a relationship between "Europe 1" and "Europe 2," the eventual resolution—presumably somewhere around the year 2000—of that issue will still leave open, and thus also place on the agenda, the question of the fate of "Europe 3." That Europe contains the Balkans, and the post-Soviet Baltic states, Ukraine, Belarus, and Moldova—of about 75 million people—and farther east, Russia itself, with its 150 million people. It is almost a tragic certainty that—unlike Central Europe, which is more likely to overcome its internal problems through its earlier association with "Europe 1"—"Europe 3," especially Russia and perhaps Ukraine as well, will be experiencing aggravated internal crises for decades to come.

Obviously, Europe will have to draw its external line more narrowly, but—however geographically defined—Europe will be faced at its very edges by major socioeconomic and probably also geopolitical turbulence. The Balkan crisis of the early 1990s—and Europe's embarrassing but symptomatic inability to respond to it—is merely an augury of the turmoil and violence that could envelop the entire eastern periphery of Europe. Russia will present Europe with an especially perplexing problem. Whatever its internal evolution, Russia will remain too large—and too "Eurasian"—to be fully integrated into Europe. Its internal problems, moreover, could spill into Europe, wherever united Europe's eastern frontiers may be set. The resulting anxieties could contaminate the European political atmosphere, become divisive in terms of policy cohesion, and are certain to accentuate European security fears.

That insecurity, compounded further by the demographic and religious challenge of nearby Islamic North Africa, will serve to sustain the European interest in an American military presence in Europe. In turn, European dependence on such continued American security presence will have the inevitable effect of inhibiting, at least to some degree, the move toward genuine political and military unity. This reality is at the root of periodic American-French tensions regarding Europe and NATO.

However, the American opposition to the French conception, and especially to the formation of a European military force based on a combined Franco-German Corps, makes longer-term sense only if one assumes an indefinite American military presence in Germany. At the moment, this assumption may appear to be justified. But one should also take into account some likely discontinuities in German popular attitudes. For one thing, Russian troops are scheduled to leave Germany in 1994. The German attitude toward the continued presence in Germany of Western troops may then change dramatically. It is almost inevitable that fewer Germans may then continue to favor Germany remaining the only country in Europe with foreign troops on its soil, with the result that the American presence may then come to be viewed as an unwelcome anachronism of the past.

It is thus historically ironic that, in effect, both America and

France are obstructing Europe's unification. America fears an economic "fortress Europe" and has strong reservations about a militarily integrated Europe outside NATO. France is right in insisting that Europe's unity requires political and military integration, and that such integration must be based on the closest political and military connection between France and Germany. But France weakens and isolates itself by insisting that the above requires Europe to assert itself against America. America, in turn, is right in insisting that the security relationship between Europe and America cannot be sustained without close cross-Atlantic political links, but America runs the risk of eventually encouraging a separate German policy—especially toward Russia—by so vigorously opposing Franco-German plans (and quietly encouraging British opposition to them) for a genuinely European political-military identity.

In any case, the debate over the future of Europe highlights the improbability of Europe organizing itself within a decade or two to become a genuine rival to America's comprehensive global power. France is too weak to lead Europe, and Germany is much too feared by other Europeans to be accepted as a leader. A consensually integrating Europe is bound to be a Europe that grows together quite slowly. It follows that for quite some time Europe will not be able to speak or act politically as a unit.

Consequently, the earlier case for a universally impacting "catalytic" Europe has to be significantly qualified. The reality is that traditional attachments, which shape European political attitudes and cultural values, will also continue to impede the projection of a coherent and positive European message of worldwide significance. Most importantly, the tolerant surface of European politics continues to hide some persistent demons. In France and Germany, the lead countries of Europe's march to unity, the potential for extremism periodically makes itself felt. Radical political parties of the left and right have been able to

obtain the support of roughly 25 percent of the French electorate. In Germany, such open mass support has been more limited,
generally not exceeding 10 percent, but outbursts of antiforeign
violence, especially after reunification, have become more frequent and the expression of xenophobic sentiments more widespread. Nationalist extremism is even stronger in the former
communist countries. It is, therefore, not yet a foregone conclusion that the age of intense European nationalism is fully over.

Thus despite the undeniable emergence in Western Europe
of a genuinely supranational European consciousness, political
tensions or economic setbacks could serve to revitalize otherwise
waning chauvinisms. This potential has already manifested itself
over the painful issue of migration. Even France, traditionally
quite open to foreign settlers and with a strong assimilationist
culture, has balked at the growing number of East Europeans
and North Africans seeking socioeconomic haven—and this has
contributed to the rise of the chauvinistically inclined National
Front. Germany likewise has felt rising popular resentments
against the influx of refugees. In a 1992 German public opinion
poll (conducted by *Der Spiegel* on April 28, 1992) the reduction
of the influx of foreigners was ranked as the number one political
issue. Similar sentiments are felt elsewhere in Europe as well.

This is not to say that Europe is sliding toward massive intolerance. By and large, democratic institutions and processes are
secure in Western Europe. Extremist nationalism is a minority
phenomenon—and, unlike the recent past, it tends to be defensive rather than offensive. Its goal is to defend the traditional
concept of the nation rather than to seek—as in the recent
past—territorial expansion. Even in Germany, which suffered
the most acute territorial losses as a consequence of two world
wars, German nationalism is not obsessed with the issue of
borders—perhaps in part because in the year 2000 most Ger-

mans are likely to be over fifty and wealthy, whereas in 1900 they were under twenty-five and poorer.

Nonetheless, Europe's ability to impact culturally and philosophically on the world at large is limited by the progressive replacement of Europe's historic universalism by a new burst of parochialism. That universalism was imperial-colonial in its political manifestation and, for a while at least, militantly Christian in its ethical-cultural manifestation. But with West European Christianity increasingly fatigued and viewed by many as a ritualistic anachronism, a secular and predominantly hedonistic mass culture—in many respects imitative of the American—is replacing the previous European self-definition as the forceful carrier and proselytizer of allegedly universal truths.

Today, most Europeans are preoccupied with the good life, defined in terms rather similar to the American consumerist ethic, expressed through political support for selectively protectionist trade barriers, reinforced by an economically paternalistic state, and increasingly devoid of any deeper philosophical content. Even though Europe, through its economic unification, is acquiring the capacity to become again a major global player, its new temples are the supermarkets and the Disneylands, and its message is more and more focused inward on self-gratification. Without spiritual vision and deprived of philosophic content, such a Europe at best can only be an echo of America.

Not surprisingly, life in a Europe incapable of proclaiming values of its own runs the risk of becoming empty and lonely. An unpublished study conducted by an Indian anthropologist of a Danish village (reported in *The Economist* of January 1, 1992) makes several points of broader relevance here. It concluded that increasingly social existence in rural Denmark—its material abundance notwithstanding—was characterized by the absence of any deeper personal ties or spiritual concerns and a pervasive loneliness—conditions not necessarily appealing to the rest of the world. Sociologists have also noted that elsewhere in Europe the pervasive sense of emptiness and preoccupation with creature comforts create a potentially incendiary state of political boredom.

A keen observer of the German scene, Theo Sommer, makes a similar point (in *Die Zeit*, May 12, 1992): "Now that growth of the German economy is confined within modest bounds the egoism of individual groups is running wild. The costs of unification are additionally fomenting selfishness." The disaffection of German taxpayers with the financial burdens inherent in the liberation and socioeconomic integration of their East German brethren bears him out. It is a reflection of the new priority of self-well-being over the once-sacred notion of patriotic sharing for the sake of national unity. The German public's unwillingness to sacrifice for its own nation is not likely to serve as the point of departure for self-denial on behalf of the even more remote global community.

German selfishness is certainly not an isolated case—as the widespread West European reluctance to open the EC's markets to the impoverished and struggling postcommunist countries of Central Europe amply demonstrates. For all the talk of a common Europe, the attitude of the West Europeans toward their recently emancipated Central European brothers has been quite unforthcoming. They have been unwilling to open wide their doors to Central European exports—so essential to Central European economic recovery—and they have insisted on maintaining discriminatory trade restrictions. Outside of German help to the former East Germany, West European aid to Central and East Europe has also been quite limited, with the West Europeans spending ten times more (about $50 billion) on subsidies for their own farmers!

The failure of Europe to react firmly to the bloodshed in the former Yugoslavia similarly reflects the combination of parochi-alism and selfishness that currently permeates the European outlook. The collapse of that multinational state produced the most bloody outbreak of sustained violence *within* Europe since 1945. But, unlike some local conflicts during the years of the Cold War, it did not pose the danger of escalation to an interna-tional collision among the superpowers. A firm reaction to the brutal "ethnic cleansings" thus entailed tolerable risks. Yet Eu-rope's posture was one of military temerity, political passivity, and social indifference. Its failure to react dramatized how long a road Europe still has to travel before it becomes a truly con-structive political force in world affairs. And it was a painful reminder that at least some of the demons of European history are still out of control.

Nonetheless, it is important to acknowledge that the emerging new Europe will still be a more peaceful Europe than in its recent past, despite the ethnic violence on its fringes and the extremist manifestations of chauvinism within some European states. It also is likely to be a less messianic Europe—in large measure because of its bitter encounters with utopian metamyths in the course of recent history. But it is in addition likely to be a Europe characterized by an inward-oriented parochialism as it lurches unsteadily toward its elusive goal of continental unity.

Such a Europe will be a less decisive force in the emerging global political process than the American microglobal commu-nity. Without a doubt, a Europe with a continental common market will be an economic giant, and in that respect it will be America's and Japan's peer. But until Europe acquires a political identity and imbues the vision of its unity with a more ambitious and globally appealing content, Europe will remain both headless and soulless.

It is, therefore, reasonable to conclude that, for some time to come, neither Brussels nor Tokyo will be able to compete with

New York City or Los Angeles as the nerve centers and style setters of the new global political process. In that respect as well as in comprehensive power, America is without true rivals. But the probability that neither Europe nor Japan will have the capacity for exercising global leadership does not automatically guarantee the continued exercise of that leadership by the United States.

Rather, *it means that the only alternative to American leadership is global anarchy while the real challenge to America's special global role increasingly comes not from without but from within. In effect, America's principal vulnerability may not be the tangible challenge of its rivals but the intangible threat posed by its own culture, which increasingly weakens, demoralizes, divides, and incapacitates America domestically, and which simultaneously attracts, corrupts, alienates, and revolutionizes the outside world.*

To be sure, America's comprehensive global power remains—and will remain for some time to come—peerless. So will the basic material attraction of the American way of life. But unlike Great Britain, which during the nineteenth century was perched on top of a slowly changing and essentially hierarchical as well as a politically passive world, American power is superimposed on a world that increasingly resembles a volcano of repressed aspirations and of an intensifying awareness of fundamental inequities. Though to the world America may today be neither faceless nor silent, long-term American ability to steer that world, while gradually defusing its explosive potential, will greatly depend on the degree to which America overcomes the impression that its own society is gradually losing the necessary moral and ethical criteria for the exercise of responsible self-control.

PART IV

Dilemmas of Global Disorder

The decisive development of our era has been the victory of the West in the protracted, forty-year-long Cold War. That victory, of America over Russia, has brought to an end the bipolar struggle for domination over world politics. But while the United States is now without a peer, with none of its rivals capable of replacing its comprehensive power, America's domestic dilemmas inhibit the physical scope of America's power and impede the translation of that power into acknowledged global authority.

As a consequence, the United States cannot be the global policeman, nor the global banker, nor even the global moralist. The first requires legitimacy, the second must be based on liquidity, and the third has to be derived from unblemished example. However, despite these limitations, the innovative— even if philosophically troubling—character of the American social system makes America the catalyst of global change. American power makes America internationally conservative, given the American stake in global stability, while the American impact makes America globally disruptive, given the destabilizing consequences of American values. This uneasy—indeed, contradictory—combination places a special burden on America: it must seek to promote international cooperation as the basis for a stable framework of world order, while at the same time it must accept the reality and even the necessity of some gradual readjustment in the distribution of global power and wealth. Thus America must be both the defender of stability and yet also the catalyst of change.

The resulting dilemma that the United States faces is the reverse of the dilemma faced by the United Nations: the UN is gradually acquiring increased global authority but it lacks effective global power. Its membership symbolizes global change— especially by representing the ever-altering global mosaic—but its structure is inflexible and has no relation to the realities of power. Moreover, its relatively recent ability to play an increasingly important role in international peacekeeping is the direct consequence of the end of the Cold War. The fact that neither Russia nor China were inclined to veto UN sponsorship of collective action—as evidenced in the Persian Gulf War of 1991 or in respect to the post-Yugoslav crisis of 1992—was derived from the unwillingness of these powers to contest the current phase of American preeminence. Should that unwillingness come to an end, the UN could quickly find itself again immobilized by the exercise of the veto power.

To be sure, the only long-term alternative to global anarchy is some form of a global confederal structure. The term "global confederation" may be a better description of what might gradually emerge than "world government," if the novel global political process assumes increasingly cooperative forms. The notion of a single world government not only evokes strongly negative reactions among those who fear that such a "government" would deprive existing nation-states of their sovereignty and would also result in an intolerant rule by a politically immature majority; it is, in any case, a misleading term because for many decades to come a single "world government" is not going to emerge. The existing nation-states are living entities, jealously protecting their identities and therefore also sovereignties, and most of them—especially the rich, advanced, and powerful ones—will not subordinate themselves to some supranational body.

However, the global political process—assuming that the forces of chaos do not come to dominate the world scene—is generating progressively deepening cooperation on a global scale. That cooperation has to assume, and is assuming, organizational forms, expressed through the growth in number and in power of international bodies, both of a functional type (such as the various multilateral organizations) and of a common cooperative and increasingly also decision-making political organ, namely the Security Council of the UN. The result is a web of institutions that cumulatively express the reality of international interdependence. That web, furthermore, is not a static but a dynamic condition: it involves a progressive expansion in the scope of the authority wielded by the various bodies, prompting the step-by-step emergence of what is in effect a rudimentary confederal governmental structure of worldwide scope.

Nonetheless, even under the best of circumstances, the translation of the global political process into truly politically effective confederal forms will take a long time—and will be subject in all probability also to occasional major reversals. In the meantime, the existing Security Council of the UN—the most important global political agency—remains handicapped by the fact that its composition no longer reflects the existing realities of global power. Moreover, it is highly unlikely that in the foreseeable future the UN might be reorganized in order to reflect more accurately such realities. Though there has been much talk of a possible permanent Security Council seat (entailing the right to exercise the veto) for Japan, any attempt at a revision of the UN Charter on behalf of Japan would open the doors to other claimants who might feel similarly entitled to such special status: Germany, India, Brazil, and Nigeria immediately come to mind. Their entry into the club of the veto-wielders would not only dilute the influence and thus the special standing of the current permanent members but would also increase the mathematical likelihood of vetoes actually being cast.

Consequently, it is probable that neither the United States nor the UN will soon be able to combine effective power with authority that is globally accepted as legitimate. The United States will continue to command the power, but its political and moral authority is likely to be disputed by significant portions of mankind; while the United Nations, even if its political and moral authority were to increase, will lack for a very long time the requisite power. In the meantime, the quest for an international order, that protects the interests of existing states while simultaneously permitting peaceful change that improves the lot of the underprivileged global majorities, will continue to be disrupted by periodic eruptions of political violence and intense social calamities. *It is a safe assumption that the interaction between the dynamics of global political awakening, the continued and in places even deepening socioeconomic crisis that already afflicts much of mankind, and the philosophic confusion inherent in the postutopian phase of contemporary history do not augur a period of historical placidity.*

The resulting principal challenges to global order involve simultaneously the geopolitical, the socioeconomic, and the ideological dimensions. The first pertains more specifically to the geopolitical consequences of the collapse of the Soviet Union, the resulting shifts in the distribution of global power, and the widening potential for regional conflicts. The second involves, above all, the crisis of the postcommunist transition, with that transition having also become in effect the test case of the relevance of modern liberal democracy. The third concerns the possibility that new worldwide ideological conflicts and power contests will arise, especially as global inequality becomes increasingly intolerable and the search for a viable social model more desperate.

ONE

The Geopolitical Vacuum

The collapse of the Soviet Union has transformed the "heartland" of Eurasia into a geopolitical vacuum. Once the lair of a mighty empire and the epicenter of a global ideological challenge, the vast space between the technologically advanced western and far eastern extremities of Eurasia has become contemporary history's black hole: its recent past is as much in dispute as is its near future. In the short run, this condition removes the security threat that the Soviet Union once posed to its richer neighbors. In the longer run, it could be the source of major and novel political dangers.

The collapse of the Soviet Union represents a significant ideological turning point—that has already been noted. But it also marks an event even more historically important: the end of the Russian Empire that existed for more than three hundred years. That empire came to dominate the largest piece of real estate in the world, and its geographical location—in the "heartland" of Eurasia—meant that its influence and power cast a shadow over that continent's western, eastern, and southern extremities. In turn, the resistance of the states located in these extremities—in recent years, with America's active involvement—defined the central geostrategic fronts of the resulting international contest.

The disappearance of the Russian Empire—assuming that it is not resurrected (on which more later)—terminates that geopolitical challenge. In the West, it means that Central Europe can gradually seek to fulfill its cultural identification with Western Europe by joining in the process of European economic and political unification. Indeed, some portions of the former empire, notably the Baltic republics and perhaps even Ukraine and Belarus, are likely to aspire in the same direction. In the Far East, the end of the empire relieves Korea, Japan, and China of the anxieties inherent in the presence on their frontiers of the massive Russian military might. Southward, Turkey, Iran, and Pakistan find themselves all of a sudden sheltered by a series of new buffer states, which reinforce the barrier separating Russia from the cherished southern warm-water ports.

Geostrategically even more important is the fact that the collapse of the heartland-based empire means that the forty-year-long effort to expel America from Eurasia is also over. The United States no longer is faced by a strategic challenge which, if successful, could have confronted America with the Eurasian continent as a whole subject to the sway of a hostile empire. To drive America back across the Atlantic and the Pacific was clearly Stalin's strategic objective in the Cold War, a goal that he shared in common with Hitler (as revealed in the secret Nazi-Soviet negotiations in late 1940 regarding the possible division of the spoils in the event of the then-anticipated victory in World War II of the Axis powers). With the Soviet Union's defeat in the Cold War and its subsequent disintegration, the United States is now able for the first time to inject its political presence in the new post-Soviet republics of Eurasia, all the way to the frontiers of China, as well as to dominate the Persian Gulf region on the southern fringes of Eurasia.

But the aftermath of the empire's disappearance is not likely to be peaceful. Unlike either the British or the French empires, in which water clearly demarcated the boundary between the home country and its colonial possessions, the Russian Empire has been a landmass without precise historically or geographically defined frontiers. The progressive expansion of that empire over several hundred years as well as the urban-industrial revolution sponsored by the Communist regime has produced large-scale Russian settlements in non-Russian lands, resulting in more than twenty-five million Russians living outside their traditional ethnic homes. Communist-forced resettlements as well as industrialization have also caused some 40 million non-Russians to find themselves outside their national homelands. That ethnic commingling is already producing increasing frictions, antagonisms, and bloodshed.

In addition to large-scale massacres, one has to anticipate multimillion migrations. Both the 25 million Russians and the 40 million non-Russians living in alien and nationalistic environments are the potential victims of political pressures for "ethnic cleansings." Their migrations will impose further strains on the socioeconomic fabric of the countries concerned, and it is also possible that they may spill over into Central Europe and even further west.

Almost every post-Soviet republic is likely to be adversely affected. By 1992 violence had already broken out in the Caucasus, involving in effect a limited but sustained ground combat between Armenia and Azerbaijan, as well as sporadic fighting within Georgia and between Georgia and Ossetia, and also in the Checheno-Ingush region. Sustained combat also developed in Moldova between Rumanian and Russian-speaking inhabitants, with elements of the Russian (the former Soviet) army directly involved. Very lethal ethnic riots also occurred in Central Asia, involving Tadzhiks, Uzbeks, Kirghizians, as well as Russian settlers. The presence of numerous Russian colonists in Latvia and Estonia has also become a source of major tension in the relationship of these states with Moscow.

It is to be expected that these problems will get worse. If the socioeconomic difficulties of the newly independent Ukraine become acute, the large Russian minority of some 10 million people (out of a total Ukrainian population of about 52 million), concentrated heavily in the key industrial regions of Kharkhov and Donetsk, may become openly disaffected. That will then tempt the Kremlin to apply pressure on Ukraine, first to obtain for this minority a special status and then perhaps even to exploit its grievances as the leverage for destabilizing Ukrainian statehood. The makings of a serious collision are inherent in this situation.

Significant violence is also a potential in the newly emancipated Moslem countries of Central Asia. It could have two foci. One might involve growing friction with the Russian settlers, who occupy in the area the better jobs and housing. Increasingly overt and probably even violent efforts to drive them out are inevitable. This is likely to be opposed by Moscow, and the Russian army could at some point become engaged, as earlier in Moldova. Even Kazakhstan, which has adopted the most accommodating posture toward Russia and the population of which has almost as many Russians as Kazakhs, is likely to experience in the relatively near future intensifying ethnic hostility, including growing violence directed at nonnatives. For the 9 million Russians living in the Central Asian region, the future looks grim.

Just as likely, and potentially even more explosive, is the possibility of ethnic and border conflicts between the newly emancipated Central Asian states. Their borders have been drawn, quite arbitrarily, by the Soviet leaders. In several cases, they have neither historic nor ethnic validity. As the new political elites assert themselves, and as the newly emancipated nationalists experience a sense of ecstatic emancipation, territorial and ethnic conflicts among them are likely to become increasingly bloody. Several extremely brutal outbreaks of ethnic violence in 1991 and 1992 foreshadow the likelihood of intensifying regional hostilities, making the Central Asian region politically very volatile.

Since nature abhors a vacuum, it is already evident that outside powers, particularly the neighboring Islamic states, are likely to try to fill the geopolitical void created in Central Asia by the collapse of Russian imperial sway. Turkey, Iran, and Pakistan have already been jockeying in order to extend their influence, while the more distant Saudi Arabia has been financing a major effort to revitalize the region's Moslem cultural and religious heritage. Islam is thus pushing northward, reversing the geopolitical momentum of the last two centuries.

From a geopolitical point of view, Russia's longer-term reaction to these developments will be decisive for the future. That reaction will determine whether Russia becomes a truly postimperial state or whether it gradually undertakes a sustained effort at imperial restoration. That choice will not be easy, for the consequences of either will be painful. The decision to abandon imperial ambitions—to emulate in some fashion the experience of Turkey after the fall of the Ottoman Empire (which in many respects was more similar to the Russian than was the overseas British Empire)—would necessitate a policy of extraordinary indifference regarding the fate of the millions of Russians living outside the frontiers of the ethnically truly Russian homeland. It is far from certain that Russian nationalism can demonstrate such forbearance, especially since Russian nationalism itself has been rekindled with new passions in the wake of the fall of Soviet communism.

Moreover, one cannot dismiss the possibility that a democratic Russia that abjures imperial ambitions may itself be prone to further fragmentation. A democratic Russia would have to accept a high degree of decentralization, given the highly varied conditions of its transcontinental economy and society. Pressures for autonomy would then be likely to grow, with the Siberian Far East increasingly oriented toward the economic miracles of Japan, Korea, and also China. The St. Petersburg region, by the same token, could be pulled through the Baltic Sea toward Scandinavia and Germany. The example of successful separatism by the non-Russian nations might lead some Russians in the above-mentioned areas to wonder why there should not be more than one or even two Russian-speaking states, just as there are more than one German-speaking or English-speaking states. Many could reason that perhaps both democracy and prosperity might thereby be more easily attainable by the Russian people.

Thus inherent in the abandonment of imperial ambitions is the prospect of further geopolitical dispersal. This is why for many Russians the reconstitution of the empire—perhaps in some new guise and in a somewhat less coercive mode—represents the more attractive option. A defensive strategy designed to preserve the outer reaches of the old Great Russian Empire may in fact be spontaneously emerging. One senses in the ongoing efforts to delay the departure of the Russian troops from the Baltic republics, to retain a strong naval base in the Kaliningrad region (of the former East Prussia), to preserve a Russian enclave on the Dniester River between Ukraine and Moldova, to entrench a Russian military presence in Crimea on the Black Sea, to fortify a protectorate in North Ossetia in the Caucasus, to reach special arrangements for mixed Russian-Turkmen and Russian-Kazakh and Russian-Tadzhik military forces on the southern frontiers of Central Asia, and to retain control over the southern Kurile islands in the Far East (even at the cost of forfeiting thereby any chance of large-scale Japanese credits), a wider design to preserve strategic posts along the outside frontiers of the former empire. That design may not be a formally calculated one; it may rather be a reflection of a deeply rooted imperial instinct—but in any case it lays the groundwork for an attempt at an eventual imperial restoration, once Russia recoups its internal cohesion and strength.

However, any such policy is also likely to generate serious conflicts, thereby guaranteeing that in one way or another the former imperial heartland is doomed to a period of turbulence and violence. The key consideration is that any Russian attempt at imperial restoration—conducted under the emotionally appealing slogan of "we must defend the millions of Russians outside of Russia"—is likely to encounter serious resistance from nationalisms that have in the meantime become awakened and have been transformed by their taste of independence. Crushing, or even undermining, their resistance will not be easy. A policy of imperial revival would thus doom Russia not only to becoming again an autocratic state but would condemn the Russian people to a protracted, spreading, and potentially even endless conflict. Russia therefore finds itself in a classical catch-22 situation.

The collapse of the Soviet Union not only creates openings for the potential projection of American influence into the Eurasian vacuum, especially through the effort to help consolidate the new non-Russian states, it also has major geopolitical consequences in the southwestern fringes of Eurasia: the Middle East and the Persian Gulf have been transformed into an area of overt and exclusive U.S. preponderance. This condition is historically unique. For much of the modern era, the region has been the object of intense big-power competition. Russia and the Ottoman Empire clashed repeatedly, as did the Ottoman Empire and Britain. After World War I, France and Britain competed for influence, with Russia lurking in the background. During World War II, the Soviet Union staked out a claim of access to the Persian Gulf but was pressured out of Iran by the United States in 1946. The Soviet military and political presence was introduced into the Middle East when the Arab states turned to Moscow for aid against Israel. It was not until the collapse of Soviet power, and especially after the Gulf War of 1991, that for the first time in modern history a single external power came to exercise exclusive preponderance.

Yet that preponderance is likely to remain quite superficial and even brittle, largely because there are no underlying bonds of shared values or political culture or religion between America and its Arab client states. American power rests largely on an alliance with local governments which, in several cases based on corrupt and obscenely rich classes, increasingly run the risk of losing touch with their own populations. Moreover, Iran is clearly an aspirant to regional hegemony and it is prepared to outwait the United States. It has an imperial tradition and possesses both the religious and the nationalist motivation to contest both the American and the Russian presence in the area. In doing so, it can count on the religious sympathy of its neighbors. With both religion and nationalism conspiring against an alien regional hegemony, the current American supremacy in the Middle East is built, quite literally, on sand.

A good illustration of the limitations of American regional control is provided by the fact that even the extraordinarily one-sided military outcome of the Gulf War of 1991 did not yield commensurate political results: Saddam Hussein's regime remained in power, and both the Shiite and Kurd revolts—despite American encouragement of them—were effectively suppressed. To have attained a political victory on a scale matching the military one would have required not only a much more costly American effort but also overcoming the very obvious reluctance even of the allied Arab states to pursue the war to the point of a politically decisive victory. This they were not willing to do, out of fear that their populations would become restive at the collusion of their own governments in a war against an Arab nation waged mostly by America.

Arab hostility toward the United States is also certain to intensify if American efforts to promote the resolution of the Arab-Israeli conflict should prove to be a failure. When the Middle East was the object of rivalry by two competing super-powers, American support of Israel could be viewed as a neces-sary expression of American self-interest as well as an act of moral obligation toward the Jewish people. But in the era of one-sided American preponderance, an American failure to pro-mote a peaceful termination of the Arab-Israeli conflict is likely to facilitate the mobilization of religious fundamentalism and nationalist radicalism against continued American regional su-premacy.

Thus, though in different ways, for Russia and America the geopolitical vacuum may become a dangerous whirlpool. The political awakening of Islam is generating not only a collision with residual Russian imperialism in the north but in time is also likely to contest American domination in the south. The former will not be able to disengage, because of its settlers and because it will feel bound to contest the intrusion into Central Asia of southern Moslem states; and the latter—while also risking intensifying hostility—will not be able to disengage because of its interest in oil and its sense of moral obligation to Israel.

The geographical perimeters of the whirlpool of violence can be drawn as an oblong on the map of Eurasia. It extends from east to west, from the Adriatic Sea next to the Balkans all the way to the border of the Chinese Sinkiang province; from south to north it loops around the Persian Gulf, embracing parts of the Middle East, then Iran, Pakistan, and Afghanistan in the

south, all of Central Asia along the Russian-Kazakh frontier to
the north, and all the way along the Russian-Ukrainian border.
The oblong thus contains portions of southeastern Europe, the
Middle East and the Persian Gulf region, in addition to the
southern sections of the former Soviet Union.

This area is composed of nearly thirty states, most in the early
stages of their own nation building. Most are yet to be politically
defined. Almost none of them are ethnically homogeneous; they
are inhabited by approximately 400 million people, and internal
violence between their several scores of ethnic groups or tribes—
often divided by language, customs, and especially religion—is
already fermenting and is bound to erupt with intensifying feroc-
ity, fueled by the growing political awakening of their peoples.
The tragedies of Lebanon of the 1980s, or of Kurdistan and the
former Yugoslavia of the early 1990s are previews of things to
come within the Eurasian oblong of maximum danger.

It is hence not a coincidence that of all the states around the
world that are acquiring or are likely before too long to acquire
weapons of mass destruction, as many as one-half are located
within this Eurasian oblong. (East Asia is emerging as the other
region engaged in the most intense acquisition of weaponry of
mass destruction.) Experts and intelligence analysts estimate
that—beyond the five openly acknowledged nuclear powers—
at least four additional states already possess a nuclear weapons
capability as well as the ballistic missiles for their delivery. Moreover, the number of states with ballistic missiles is already fifteen
or so. Most of these states also have ongoing offensive biological
and/or chemical warfare programs. This total is expected at least
to double by the year 2000.

The proliferation of weapons of mass destruction is now a
reality. Under the current circumstances, in which U.S. global
power lacks the commensurate authority and in which the UN's
global authority lacks the needed power, only a delaying action
is feasible. The agreement concluded by twenty-seven states in

April of 1992 designed to limit the sale of dual-use machinery and materials suitable for the production of nuclear weapons is a case in point. Some potential nuclear supplier states did not sign it (notably China), and though the agreement provides for comprehensive scrutiny of some sixty-five classes of dual-use technology—and thus, in theory, it could inhibit proliferation— its enforcement is entirely voluntary. Significant evasion is almost certain.

Within the oblong of maximum danger, violence could erupt among a variety of parties in a great variety of combinations. The list of potential conflicts is dismayingly long: they could occur between differing ethnic groups inhabiting the states of the region; or between Russia and some of the new Central Asian states, the latter perhaps supported by one or more of the established Moslem states to the south; or between some of the new Central Asian states, with differing Islamic sponsors in the background; or even between Russia and Ukraine, especially if internal economic problems in Ukraine were to prompt secessionist aspirations among its large Russian minority; or between some of the Balkan states, perhaps even involving Greece and Turkey; or between Israel and an Arab state; or between Iran and some Persian Gulf states and/or the United States; or between Iraq and also the foregoing; or, of course, between India and Pakistan. One cannot exclude also the possibility of some Chinese involvement in the Central Asia conflicts, especially if they should involve areas next to China, and in any major new Indian-Pakistani collision.

The list, certainly not exhaustive, points to two major probabilities: 1. At some point, weapons of mass destruction are likely to be used, especially given the ethnic and religious passions involved in some of the possible conflicts; 2. Effective restraint through some form of international sanction could be inhibited if it became known that the parties to the conflict possessed and were fanatical enough to employ such weaponry. Such knowledge would have a chilling effect on the ardor for international peace-enforcement of the democratic and comfortably richer publics.

These dangers could be minimized if consensus existed among the members of the existing nuclear "club"—all of whom are permanent members of the UN Security Council— to act in unison against any would-be employer of weapons of mass destruction. Such consensus, however, is not likely in regard to the most probable outbreaks of major warfare in the Eurasian oblong. On the contrary, dissent would then probably ensue among the five, thereby paralyzing the Security Council. In such circumstances, the only remaining deterrent would be a willingness by the United States to undertake unilateral and massive military action, perhaps even pledged in advance against any state that initiated the use of weapons of mass de- struction against any other state. It is doubtful, however, that the U.S. Congress would be willing to commit America to a generalized and blanket obligation with such far-reaching con- sequences. It is also not certain that the international commu- nity would endorse such a special "policeman" role for the United States.

James Schlesinger was therefore undoubtedly correct when he concluded in early 1992 that "The world order of the future . . . will be marked by power politics, national rivalries, and ethnic tensions." And, one may add, also by the likelihood that weapons of mass destruction will at some point be used in the world's geopolitical vortex of violence.*

---

* As this book was in press, I had the opportunity to read the unpublished—and highly compelling—essay by Samuel P. Huntington of Harvard University entitled "The Clash of Civilizations?" In it, he makes a powerful case that conflicts along the fault lines of what he defines as the Islamic, Confucian, and Christian civilizations will pose in the future the major threat to world peace. This book's discussion on pp. 163–65 of "the oblong of violence" deals, in effect, with the geographical vortex of Huntington's clashing civilizations. See also p. 198 below.

TWO

The Vengeful Phoenix

The foregoing highlights the need for effective international solidarity in order to contain the destructive dynamics of global instability. However, two major developments are likely to inhibit the emergence of the international solidarity that is so needed as the foundation for an effective world order. The first involves the prospects for postcommunist transition, and that impinges especially on the future role of Russia. The second pertains to the dilemmas of global inequality, and that bears heavily on the future role of China.

The postcommunist transition currently affects several hundred million people. It is being undertaken, by necessity, without either a guiding concept or an exemplary model. The postcommunist reformers are, in effect, pioneers in virgin territory. No major study of contemporary economics or of comparative politics contains any systematic analysis or prescription of how to transform a statist, initially revolutionary and later corrupt totalitarian system into a pluralistic democracy based on a free market system. As a clever observer once put it, there are recipes for making an omelette out of eggs but no recipe for making eggs

167

out of an omelette. And so far there is also no actual model—
that is, no precedent of relevant historical experience—on which
to base a comprehensive, long-term policy for a successful transformation.

To be sure, before too long, the former East Germany is
likely to become the showcase of a successful postcommunist
transition. It is to be expected that by the year 1995 wage levels
between the two formerly divided parts of Germany will have
been equalized (naturally at West German levels), and by the
year 2000 the inhabitants of the former East Germany will enjoy
a standard of living matching that of the rest of Germany. East
Germany is then likely to be acclaimed as the successful example.
However, in this regard, one major—indeed, centrally decisive—consideration needs to be registered: the former East Germany is not being transformed as a separate nation and a separate
economy, but as a province of a much larger nation-state. It is
being assimilated into Europe's most dynamic economy, one that
has been able to pump into the former East Germany of only 16
million people approximately $100 billion per year—and, even
so, the effort is encountering major difficulties and is producing
rising social tensions in the ex-communist state.

No even remotely comparable flow of capital to any of the
other former communist states is to be expected. Perhaps in
time, Central Europe—especially either Poland or Hungary—
may provide, through trial and error and with the help of a much
more modest inflow of external capital, the needed model. But
several reservations immediately come to mind. Hungary is too
small a country to offer a viable example for much of the former
Soviet bloc, and especially for the vast, continental Russia. Its
small size and proximity to the West facilitate a Western-assisted
transformation. Poland, with its nearly 40 million people, comes
closer to becoming a model, if its efforts—the boldest and most
ambitious of the former communist states—eventually prove

successful. But Poland and the rest of Central Europe suffered under communism only for slightly over forty years; Poland was never fully communized economically (with private agriculture and with some services and retail trade remaining in private hands) nor ideologically (with a strong and independent Catholic church defying the Marxist doctrines), and moreover Central Europe has had long-standing ties with Western Europe.

By contrast, in Russia communism endured for three-quarters of a century. It was more indigenous and took deeper roots, impacting much more on the collective psyche of the people, conditioning both their political as well as their socioeconomic culture. The difficulties of the challenge are thus much greater in the former Soviet Union, the stakes much higher, and the scale more immense. The postcommunist transformation there affects some 300 million people, and the failure or success of the democratic option will have major international significance—including for the less developed and still economically struggling countries. Indeed, that transformation has to be seen as the final act in the great ideological struggles of the twentieth century.

The role of Western aid in that transformation is bound to be much less significant than in the case of East Germany or even Central Europe. To match what the East German population has been obtaining would require for several years the *annual* transfer to Russia, which by itself accounts for about 150 million people of the former Soviet Union, of almost $1000 billion, a sum that is only useful as a measurement of the relative insignificance to Russia's transformation of the amounts that have actually been flowing from the West as of the early 1990s. The bottom line is that—though Western aid is needed and should be forthcoming—the reconstruction of Russia, and especially its postcommunist transformation, will have to be largely an effort conducted by the Russians themselves.

That effort, lacking either established concepts or models,

will have to take into account the specific Russian legacies of
communism—not in order to perpetuate them but in order to
get rid of them in a manner that is conducive to the emergence
of a stable and increasingly democratic political system while
also promoting a more decentralized and increasingly market-
based economy. The wording used in the preceding sentence is
deliberately meant to convey that the process involved in seeking
both objectives will have to be gradual. The fact is that in Russia—unlike, for example, in Poland—the entrepreneurial tradition has been almost extinguished and private enterprise
extirpated. The communist legacy is a Russian society with little
understanding of the financial and competitive intricacies of the
free market and a statist economy saddled with a huge and
inefficient heavy industrial sector.

In these circumstances, an attempt by Russia to imitate the
headlong rush of the Poles toward a market economy could
generate a fatal contradiction between the political goal of democracy and the economic goal of the free market. This is
so because postcommunist Russia lacks the social and political
institutions capable of instilling and sustaining social discipline
in the inevitably painful phase of economic disruption, inherent
in the necessary restructuring of the economy. The Orthodox
church does not enjoy the organizational and spiritual authority
of the Polish Catholic church, and no nationwide organization
dedicated to contesting communist power (like Poland's Solidarity movement) emerged either during the abortive "perestroika"
or even in the final months of the Soviet system's agony. Arkadiy
Volskiy, chairman of the Russian Union of Industrialists and
Entrepreneurs, an opponent of rapid change, drew attention to
these contrasts when he noted (in an interview with *Novoye
Vremya*, July 1992) that "people here are fond of referring to the
Polish experience and to shock therapy. But one must not bank
on shock therapy in Russia: by dint of our habit of taking every-

thing to extremes, shock therapy here would become shock surgery. And generally speaking, Polish society is far more consolidated—95 percent are practicing Catholics. Cardinal Glemp was able to raise his finger and say: No strikes! And there weren't any. 'Solidarity' also united society. The government had 'feet' which it planted on the ground. There was support from below." Social hardships and economic deprivation imposed by very rapid privatization would hence be much more likely to generate massive and politically destabilizing unrest in Russia than has been the case in Poland.

To instill in the former Soviet Union the needed entrepreneurial ethic and to privatize the existing economic system will take years—in fact, several decades—of sustained and very patient effort. Haste will not only make waste but is likely to plunge Russia into a revolutionary situation. This would be especially likely if large-scale unemployment were generated by an indiscriminate policy of rapid privatization and/or bankruptcy of Russia's major industrial enterprises. The basic reality is that even under the best of circumstances, very large segments of Russia's industry cannot be privatized because they are uncompetitive, while closing them down abruptly would mean unleashing unemployment on the scale of tens of millions. The situation is just as unpromising in agriculture. With the Russian peasantry decimated and the collective/state farms made dependent on machinery suited only for large-scale farming, decollectivization is not likely to attract many would-be private farmers and economically it would probably even be a failure.

Thus it would be historically ironic if the failures of communist dogmas were to prompt the post-Communist Russian leadership to adopt in a simplistic and mechanical fashion a new dogma of the free market, without regard for the social costs and political risks involved. Yet, by and large, that has been the advice that has been flowing to Russia from the West. Russia has been persistently urged to build democracy and to create a free market, both at the same time. That advice is being absorbed, and even dogmatized, by an elite that has relatively little grasp of the sensitive connection between culture and economics, and one which tends to invoke the words "free market" with the same ritualistic formalism with which their predecessors were proclaiming their devotion to "the construction of socialism."

Instead, the post-Communist Russian leadership might well be advised to give a higher priority to the institutionalization and consolidation of firm constitutional and democratic processes, so that a stable political framework could absorb the unavoidable shock effects of far-reaching socioeconomic changes. *Until— and unless—a structure of laws, a system of political parties, and stable parliamentary procedures are effectively established, the pursuit simultaneously of the goals of democracy and of the free market can prove to be mutually self-defeating.* As of 1992, only one truly democratically elected official in all of Russia—its president, Boris Yeltsin—was undertaking to promote basic changes in a deeply rooted but massively corrupt and inefficient system, in a setting of political quasi-anarchy. Without a firm constitutional state, the likely social backlash could get out of hand and be exploited by forces inimical both to democracy and the free market.

In addition, the Russian leadership might also benefit from a closer look at the post–World War II experience of some Asian states in steering their national economic development. The successful Asian states recognized that, to catch up with the free market front-runners, some degree of prolonged governmental intervention was necessary, especially in providing long-term policy consistency through the deliberate definition of national economic objectives. In addition, governments had to assume a major role in promulgation of policies designed to enhance the social and physical infrastructure, which the free market by itself was less likely to do. Last but not least, the Russians need to understand—in the words of the leading Japanese planner, Saburo Okita—that "market mechanisms are not infallible," especially in formerly communist countries, because their economies "need still government intervention not only to offset market failures, but also because their private sector economies are less mature and their markets underdeveloped."

But whatever economic policy the post-Communist Russian leadership pursues, the political and economic prospects for Russia in the near term are in any case fundamentally unfavorable. Communism has ravaged both the Russian soul and the Russian body to such an extent that any recovery will be prolonged, painful, with the outcome more than uncertain. The near-term prospects are especially grim, with growing evidence that Russia is beginning to experience socioeconomically a decline in many ways comparable to the American Great Depression of the early 1930s: a dramatic drop in production and consumption, hyperinflation, and increasing unemployment. The country also faces the prospect of intensifying class conflicts—with the increasingly poor masses tempted to vent their jealousy of the few newly rich—and deepening political hatreds. In that setting, the Russian people are not likely to absorb either the entrepreneurial spirit nor the political culture of compromise needed for a successful transformation into a democratic and economically pluralistic system. The resulting casualties might well be both the free market and the incipient Russian democracy.

An intensifying crisis of the Russian spirit is the inevitable product of the deepening economic crisis and of the geopolitical fragmentation of the Russian Empire. That crisis makes the Russian people more susceptible to extreme political viewpoints, and it is already generating a polarizing debate about the future external and internal destiny of Russia. With the crumbling of the Russian Empire, what is "Russia"? What does it now mean to be a "Russian"? Are these ethnic or supranational concepts (similar to the distinction between the "English" nation and the wider notion of the "British" people)? Disillusion with democratic slogans and disappointment with the new economic order are making the population yearn even more for some new verities, to fill the void left by the disappearance of communism and by the growing disenchantment with liberalism.

One should not underestimate the potential implications of this mood. The Russian people have always had a special quasi-religious and quasi-philosophical sense of their historical destiny. The notion of Moscow as the Third Rome was not some idle slogan; it was the expression of a deeply internalized sense of special mission. That is what made the transplantation of communist universalism to the Russian soil for a while so appealing: it gave the people a sense of an even more universal vocation, one which extended beyond the confines of the old Russian Empire. *Ex oriente, lux*—that phrase, often cited, actually was deeply meaningful, especially to the Russian intellectuals, with their proclivity for groping for transcendental formulas which would define reality in terms of an absolute truth. Russia, in their view, was destined to be the carrier of that "light," redeeming the corrupt West from its pervasive depravity. In turn, the sense of mission and the related faith could justify for the Russians the requisite personal sacrifices, including the humble submission of the individual—of his/her own free will—to a grander calling.

Connected to all that was the genuine sense of pride in great power status. Russia was a mighty power. It had been such for about three hundred years. Whether as the seat of power for the Tsarist empire or more recently for the Soviet Union, the Kremlin presided over the destiny not only of a great nation but of many directly subordinated peoples. More generally, it impacted on world affairs, and everyone in the world had to listen carefully to what the Kremlin was saying. Politically conscious Russians derived both pride and status from that condition. In more recent years, the Soviet Union saw itself as the coequal rival to the United States, it measured itself by the competition with America, and it saw itself—on the basis of the Marxist doctrines of historical inevitability—as destined to supplant the United States in external power and internal well-being.

The fall of the Soviet Union and the disintegration of the Russian Empire has thus been a profound shock even to those Russians who came to recognize the fallibility of their Marxist doctrine and the inner hypocrisy and operational inefficiency of the Soviet system. All of a sudden, a truncated Russia has been demoted to the status of a poor and dependent "Third World" country, the beneficiary of Western advice and charity, and the object of ridicule and repudiation by its formerly subject non-Russian peoples. This is a condition that rankles many. And for the masses at large that condition is expressed tangibly through the sudden onset of intense social deprivations, made even more intolerable by mounting evidence of internal chaos.

What vision of the future is then likely to prove appealing and compelling? A minority makes the strong case that Russia should become a normal, postimperial, and increasingly European nation-state. They advocate, in effect, the eventual incorporation of Russia in the emerging European community (initially, perhaps, confederation), and therefore also the permanent acceptance by Russia of the separate independence of its former non-Russian subjects. In their vision, Russia is to become what Poland is in the process of becoming (and culturally has always seen itself as being): a European state that is an integral part of the common and larger European civilization. Admittedly, this will be a slow process—for the objective and subjective gaps separating Russia from the West remain enormous—but in the view of the advocates of this perspective there is no other way for Russia to become both modern and democratic.

But to many that view is both impractical as well as perverse. It is impractical because for many decades to come Russia will not be able to close the gaps in the standard of living and in the way of thinking that separate Russia from Europe. It is perverse, for it would in any case entail the repudiation by Russia of its own distinctive culture, history, and "soul." Becoming part of Europe would mean ceasing to be distinctively Russian, for in the view of those who reject the European option, Russia is not just another nation-state but a distinctive and truly alternative way of life, a civilization of its own, an identity to be recognized in the same degree that "Europe" and "Asia" are also distinctive (even if difficult precisely to define) identities.

Symptomatic of these clashing perspectives has been the debate in Moscow that has been gaining in intensity as of 1992. At first, the collapse of the Soviet Union left the field open to those who have come to represent the Western or the European orientation. They have dominated the public discourse on the future of Russia in the phase of the postcommunist transition. But slowly, with the domestic difficulties of that transition gradually generating growing doubts about the liberal formula and the Western prescription, voices have started to surface, arguing that Russia's external and internal orientation ought to be different, more distinctive, and more in keeping with Russia's specific traditions and interests.

These alternative perspectives range from the moderate to the extreme. But they have certain themes in common. In their moderate variant, they involve the rejection of both the above orientations, stressing that "Russia's mission in the world . . . is to initiate and support a multilateral dialogue of cultures, civilizations, and states. Russia the conciliator, Russia connecting, Russia combining. . . . A country imbibing West and East,

North and South, unique and exclusively capable, perhaps, of the harmonious combination of many different principles, of a historic symphony." These words by Sergei Stankevich (*Nezavisimaya Gazeta*, March 28, 1992), himself a democratically oriented politician, are revealing in that they still reflect the special sense of the Russian mission in the world, a mission that is derived from uniqueness and entails a special calling.

The practical conclusion that was drawn from the above was that Russia should increasingly stake out for itself a special global position, seeking leadership among the world's developing countries. At home, the above viewpoint stressed enhanced emphasis on Russia's obligation and right to defend the Russians living outside of Russia's natural frontiers. "A tougher tone" has been explicitly advocated, with Russia urged to assert vigorously its "right" to side with "the undeservedly insulted and unjustly persecuted"—which the ongoing government of Russia was accused of failing to do.

The above, it is to be noted, represents the moderate alternative. But much more strident Russian voices are also increasingly being heard, deploring both the collapse of the internal empire and the allegedly excessive pro-Western orientation of the post-communist Russian leaders. In their view, the domestic policy ought to aim at the recreation of the "union" (a euphemism for the empire), for example, with Yevgeniy Ambartsumov (chairman of the Supreme Soviet Committee for International Affairs) flatly declaring that "I am more and more convinced that the breakup of the USSR was a totally ill-considered, irresponsible step," the restoration of which "will, unfortunately, not be painless" (*Rossiyskaya Gazeta*, April 13, 1992).

That restoration is becoming increasingly the openly articulated goal of the political rivals to Russia's President Boris Yeltsin. His vice-president, Aleksandr Rutskoy, has made a vocation out of appeals to Russian pride and of denunciations of the negative consequences of the collapse of Russia's imperial power. That collapse is increasingly described as the root cause of Russia's internal socioeconomic difficulties, compounded by the allegedly excessive deference of the new Kremlin rulers to Western desires. Rutskoy has adopted a particularly strident position toward Ukrainian independence, deploring the separation of the Russian and Ukrainian peoples and urging a policy of sustained pressure against Kiev. In doing so, he repeatedly— in frequent speeches and widely disseminated articles—invokes memories of past Russian glory, eulogizing Russia's imperial exploits, in an evident attempt to evoke a popular echo from the messianic and missionary instincts of his audiences.

Given Russia's growing internal difficulties, it is not surprising that demagogic politicians are increasingly tempted to develop a comprehensive indictment of postcommunist policies, presenting the collapse of the empire and the pro-Western orientation of the Yeltsin government as the root causes of political chaos and economic degradation. Democracy at home and accommodation abroad thus become the increasingly openly articulated targets. Vladimir Zhirinovskiy, who obtained some 7 million votes in the 1991 elections for the office of Russia's president, has gone the furthest in presenting publicly a program for the adoption of a statist authoritarianism at home and for the restoration of the empire beyond Russia's national boundaries. He has also called for a policy in which Russia identifies itself explicitly with the poorer countries of the south, where it can play a leading role, rather than seeking to become a poor member in the club of the rich.

The important point to bear in mind is that the extreme point of view associated with politically isolated individuals like Zhirinovskiy is gradually seeping into the rhetoric and vocabulary of more democratically minded political leaders, like Rutskoy or Stankevich, who once were closely associated with the anticommunist upheaval of 1991. The effect is to reinforce Russian geopolitical skepticism regarding the viability of the "European" orientation and to tempt Russia with either a Third World option or even—as some have vaguely advocated—with seeking an anti-Western accommodation of some sort with the Islamic wave from the south. For the Russian public at large—itself increasingly disaffected with the status quo, thoroughly confused by the new economic procedures, alienated from the much-envied but unattainable Western culture (which it therefore becomes increasingly fashionable to denounce for its materialistic hedonism), and yearning for some new verity—statist nationalism thereby becomes the only unifying ideological alternative.

That nationalist appeal does not imply a return to communism. That option has become too discredited, too many Russians have suffered directly under Stalinism, and too many horrifying revelations from the past have suffused the Russian media to permit a renewed and explicitly communist option. But a concept of the strong state that embodies the unique traditions of Russia, that imposes discipline in the name of a higher ideal, that seeks to regain global recognition for a powerful empire, and that defines for itself a new mission in regard to the outside world—perhaps in conjunction with other deprived states—can be highly appealing. It can clear away the philosophic confusion that today clouds the mind of the average Russian; it can again define reality in clear-cut black and white terms and can provide a justification for social sacrifice and political submission.

The ultimate danger is that this points toward a new mobilizing metamyth. But that danger is unlikely to manifest itself in the shape of a resurrected communism, but rather as a new form of fascism. Fascism is particularly effective in exploiting the irrational side of human nature, appealing quite effectively to emotions that can be galvanized through nationalistic symbols, exploiting the attraction of national power and glory, and responding to the craving for discipline and uniformity. Communism in its theoretical manifestations both expects too much of the human being and misjudges the basic instincts that drive human conduct. As a doctrine, fascism is much more primitive, but as an emotion, fascism is more basic, elemental, and potent.

A Russian variant of fascism is unlikely to go quite as far as nazism, with its unique racial obsessions. Unlike communism or nazism, Russian fascism would express itself through authoritarianism rather than totalitarianism, through chauvinism rather than ideology, and through statism rather than collectivism. It would not even have to proclaim itself to be fascism or embrace overtly the earlier Fascist doctrines. More likely, it would be fascism primarily in practice: the combination of dictatorial rule, state domination over a partially private economy, chauvinism, and emphasis on imperial myths and mission. That mixture would then fill the void of the black hole that bolshevism created in Russia, creating the conditions of coercive order—even if no longer of coercive utopia—that democracy and the free market may not have been able to ensure.

The reincarnation of a form of fascism, if it should ultimately occur, is not likely to be confined to Russia alone. It would almost certainly spread to some of the non-Russian former Soviet republics, whose internal difficulties are likely to be no less intense and whose democratic prospects are even bleaker than Russia's. It could also infect the politically more unstable portions of Central Europe, especially if the postcommunist transformation in that region were to falter, and even spread to some portions of Western Europe. The rebirth of fascism, more generally, would represent the defeat of the pluralistic and pragmatic vision of reality which rejects the notion that certainty, unanimity, and discipline from the top down are the hallmarks of a healthy society.

The reincarnation of the Fascist phoenix in Russia would not only represent a supreme historical irony. With its potential for contagion, a new form of fascism would also pose a vengeful challenge to the quest for international cooperation. It would represent a catastrophically infectious failure of the democratic alternative as the path to the future, while a nationalistically motivated Russia, driven by a renewed imperial instinct and thus most likely engaged in intensifying conflicts with its neighbors, would inevitably become a destructive force contributing to a world increasingly unable to control its destiny.

THREE

The Giant of Global Inequality

For most of world history, inequality was tolerated because continents were separated by huge distances and characterized by cultural remoteness. In a world that has become proximate and more intimate, and which is characterized by a massive political awakening, inequality is becoming less tolerable. How that rejection of inequality will be expressed depends, however, on whether it acquires a defined sense of direction and an accepted leadership. This raises the question not only of Russia's future role but of China's.

The fact that the new sense of proximity makes for intensified awareness of inequality in the global condition of life is a decisively important new aspect of our contemporary reality. The spread of political consciousness stimulates an intensifying rejection of that condition. For some time to come, the rejection may be inchoate, expressed more through resentment than through organized action, but it is almost certain to permeate increasingly the outlook of the vast majority of mankind that is aware of, and envies, the hedonistic cornucopia of the wealthy few. As a result, global inequality is bound to become a major issue of twenty-first-century politics.

Democracy, based on the free market system, appears to be currently triumphant. But its triumph is derived more from the failure of communism than from the successful demonstration of the viability of democratic ideals under all and any circumstances. To much of the poorer world, that case is yet to be made on the practical level of life. Procedural freedom, without substantive freedom from basic wants, may not be enough—while the cultural hedonism of the West may appear to be less proof of the inherent superiority of the free market and more the consequence of wider global inequality. That is why the victory of democracy in the ideological conflict is still more the victory of the American-led coalition over the Soviet bloc than a universal triumph of the ideas themselves. *To be sure, the ideological content of the victory is undeniable, but the global sweep of that victory is philosophically superficial.*

In the meantime, both objective and subjective forces are elevating the issue of equality into the forefront of the next century's agenda. The objective factors are derived from the dynamics of demography and economics. Global demographic growth is highly uneven, affecting much more the poorer portions of mankind. Economic growth is also uneven, but it favors the richer portions of mankind. Thus, as the population of the world grows, the disproportion in the distribution of the world's wealth becomes even more marked. According to most experts, the population of the world will be near 7 billion by the year 2000 (having more than quadrupled from 1.5 billion in 1900) and will reach 8.5 billion by 2025. Of that total, as many as 6.5 billion are likely to be living in the poorer states of mankind, with such states as Bangladesh having grown from their current 115 to 235 million, Egypt from 50 to 125 million, Kenya from

24 to 80 million, and India from 855 to 1,440 million. Even worse, approximately two-thirds of these will be concentrated in the urban slums of the less developed world, making them highly susceptible to radical political mobilization.

Negative demographic trends are reinforced by negative economic trends. According to the United Nations Development Program's "Human Development Report" for 1992, in the 1960s the richer countries were thirty times wealthier than the poorer ones, but by the 1990s the gap had widened to the point that the income of the former had become 150 times higher! That process is not being reversed. It is also occurring within the poor countries themselves, sharpening their internal social cleavages. The report also estimates that the poorer portions of the disadvantaged countries actually are obtaining, on a per capita basis, only one-half of the aid that is flowing at the same time to the somewhat more advantaged portions of the developing world. Finally, the rates of economic growth have been consistently higher in the developed or more successfully developing portions of mankind, thereby further widening the objective gap.

The resentment against that gap will be intensified on the subjective level by the disproportions that are opening up in the aging process. That portion of the populations of the rich countries who are over the age of sixty-five is increasing much more rapidly than the corresponding age bracket in the poorer countries, while their number under the age of fifteen is shrinking more rapidly. The existence of a large, volatile, often unemployed or underemployed and almost certainly impoverished mass of restive young people—but a mass aware through modern communications of the conditions prevailing elsewhere and increasingly politically activated—will enhance the impatience and frustration that is likely to become pervasive in the underprivileged portions of the globe.

In the meantime, and perhaps unexpectedly, the growing concern in the richer parts of the world with the ecological dimension is likely to reinforce the increasing centrality of the equality issue. The ecological problem is a very serious one, ultimately threatening all of humanity. It, therefore, deserves urgent attention. It has been neglected for far too long. But the fact must be faced that the most egregious offenders so far have been the developed nations. It is in Europe and in North America that a number of species have already been wiped out in their entirety and it is in these areas that extensive deforestation has taken place. The developed nations, and especially the former communist ones, have industrialized with little regard for the environment, with consequences that are beginning seriously to endanger human life. It is their policies that have produced the atmospheric concentrations of heat-trapping carbon dioxide that threaten through uncontrolled buildup a global catastrophe.

The developing countries are emulating the historical experience of the richer ones through an often reckless industrialization, not because they are indifferent to ecological concerns; they are doing so because such emulation is for them the only way of eradicating the backwardness and poverty from which they suffer. It is, in their view, the lesser evil. Moreover, they feel that the richer parts of the world cannot escape their share of responsibility simply by pleading that in the years past the world as a whole was unaware of the ecological dimension and that, therefore, the manner in which the developed world industrialized is a closed book and thus not part of the calculus of the cost of coping with environmental problems. In brief, in their view the rich portions of mankind bear both a higher responsibility for the gravity of the problem and a higher obligation to shoulder most of the financial burden.

Concerns over global ecology thus dramatize the mounting salience of the problem of global equality. Such concerns have become especially powerful in the advanced states, and within them among the upper social classes. This, as of itself, does not disqualify their substantive legitimacy, even though there is a touch of social fashion to them. (It is also precipitating a lively debate among scientists: is the concern over ecology generating a new "ism"—that of an "irrational ecologism," as some have charged—and can one seriously argue that ecological decisions should be made exclusively on the basis of so-called scientific criteria, to the exclusion of political considerations?) But inherent in the embrace of ecology by the richer side of humanity is also a contradiction between the new passion for nature and the cornucopian life-style of a significant portion of the more privileged. Unless their life-style itself is subjected to considerable reevaluation, including the adoption of far-reaching self-control regarding the satisfaction not of real wants but of self-gratifying desires, the emphasis on ecology could become yet another intensifier of the conflict between the rich and the poor.

To some extent, it has already become so. The frictions manifested at the Rio Conference of 1992 were but the superficial expression of a deeper and widening gulf. Moreover, to the extent that the richer countries are increasingly inclined to concentrate on their environmental problems at home, the prospects are that the gap in the quality of life between the rich and the poor will further widen. Some critics of the NAFTA (North American Free Trade Area) have argued that it will permit American business to ravage the Mexican environment while making it easier to protect America's. America is already spending over 2 percent of its GNP on safeguarding and restoring its ecology, Germany is approaching that ratio, and other advanced countries are moving in the same direction. The sums involved will soon be in the neighborhood of about $200 billion a year. At some point, the question will inevitably arise as to whether a major portion of that amount should not be used in an international effort not only to protect the environment but also more generally to improve the lot of the poorer states.

In time, among the richer portions of mankind, the concern for ecology may thus prove to be a catalyst for greater recognition of the need both for a philosophical reassessment of its way of life and for enhanced attention to the dilemmas of socioeconomic inequality. The failure of communism has dimmed the relative importance of the West's agenda of the latter issue. However, the genuine fear that life may be threatened by continued indifference to the ongoing destruction of the environment—a fear inevitably stronger among those who enjoy to a greater extent the fruits of life—might drive the advanced world toward policies that do, in fact, begin to address these larger socioeconomic dilemmas. This is all the more probable since a politically awakening world is less and less likely to tolerate massive disproportions in the conditions of life.

The issue of equality is already generating increased attention from the world's major religions. Over the centuries, the great religions have been quite naturally concerned with the question of social justice and their focus has been on the poor. But while exhorting the rich to be more compassionate toward the poor, essentially they have tended to preach passivity and acceptance rather than reform and change. As institutions, they have been driven by the imperatives of reality to make their accommodations with the powerful and the rich. In time, and in spite of themselves, they have tended to become reinforcements of the status quo, notwithstanding their genuine moral concerns and the self-sacrificial sense of mission that has motivated those who have dedicated their lives to religious vocation.

However, faced with growing secularism, threatened by the modern life-style, and repelled morally by the hedonistic mass culture of the West, both Christianity and Islam are becoming more absorbed by the issue of equality as the spiritually defining

dilemma of modern life. In doing so, they may partially fill the
void left by Marxism, but in a different manner. Communism
focused on inequality from a materialistic perspective, rejecting
the centrality of the spiritual dimension, and arguing that it
would succeed in creating a material life of well-being for all,
with the human being motivated and defined by materialistic
drives. The religions instead stress that the good life is defined,
first of all, in spiritual terms, and that the real meaning of the
good life involves the imperative of justice in human relations.
The quest for equality should not be expressed mechanistically
through the equalization of material possessions but should serve
as the point of departure for self-restraint in material acquisi-
tions and for the expression of mutual responsibility.

The Catholic church, the most powerful branch of contemporary Christianity, has more and more been pointing at what it
considers the negative cultural manifestations of capitalism: its
preoccupation with individual material and sensate self-gratification, regardless of social consequences. Papal encyclicals and
exhortations, while accepting the productive efficiency of the
free market, have been sharp in their denunciation of the moral
depravity inherent in a culture that places the satisfaction of all
and any individual desires above social responsibility and of the
dangers inherent in a market—including the role in it of the
mass media—that competes in the constant stimulation of such
desires. By emphasizing instead the overall quality of life, and
especially the need for a harmonious balance between the spiritual and the material dimensions of life, the church has been
highlighting the issue of socioeconomic inequality as one that
must be addressed on an urgent basis.

As a practical matter, Catholicism, and other Christian
churches as well, realize that it is in the poorer areas of the world
that their mission has the highest calling. It is in Latin America
and in some parts of Africa and Asia that religious faith is

still deeper and more alive, and the prospects for successful proselytisms most promising. They must, therefore, focus on the issues that inevitably galvanize the political and social preoccupations of the people. Preaching the spiritually ennobling humility of acceptance thus no longer suffices. Instead, the definition of the spiritually meaningful life becomes increasingly, in the poorer regions, the progressive eradication of poverty and, in the richer regions, the adoption of self-restraint in the quest for material rewards. Christianity, which has always emphasized spiritual equality and even the spiritual superiority of poverty over wealth, is thus driven toward a more active rejection of deepening material inequality.

However, the church is careful not to prescribe any particular social model. In the words of Vatican II, "Human rights norms do not lead to the prescription of any single economic, political, or ideological system. . . . Rather, basic human rights set limits and establish obligations for all systems and ideologies, leaving the precise form in which these systems will be organized undefined." Moreover, the church abjures revolutionary violence as the means of achieving social justice. When the Latin American bishops adopted the famous formula of "the preferential option for the poor," Pope John Paul II—in endorsing it in 1979—also stressed that the mission of the church "consists in complete salvation through a transforming, peacemaking, pardoning, and reconciling love." Nonetheless, the commitment was clearly made and in 1992, despite some intervening efforts to focus concern more on the dangers of modern culture and secularism, the pope, at a meeting with the Latin American bishops, with some passion reaffirmed the centrality of "the preferential option for the poor."

The same, in a somewhat more indirect manner, is the case with the other major proselytizing religion, Islam. Although traditionally viewed as inclined much more than Christianity toward a fatalistic acceptance of reality, contemporary Islam is becoming a motivating force for the rejection of inequality through its repudiation of Western-type modernity. Viewing that modernity as fundamentally corrupt and as driven by a cultural capitulation to the most basic sensate impulses, Islamic thinkers are attempting to develop the concept of an Islamic modernity that would permit Moslem societies to enjoy the technological fruits of modernity minus its cultural handicaps. In doing so, they hark back to that phase of Islamic history—some centuries ago—during which the world of Islam was simultaneously the world of innovative knowledge and of pioneering science. In that manner, their attempt at Islamic sociophilosophical renovation becomes also associated with the effort to undo what many Moslems perceive to be a state of cultural and political inequality in relation to the preponderant West.

In effect, in the Islamic world a more cohesive as well as more assertive religious orientation is generating a defensive outlook, determined to exclude the "corruptive" influence of the West while seeking to promote both the revival and the renewal of the long-dormant Moslem civilization. Religion and politics are thus combining in an effort to provide an Islamic alternative, in which technological but not cultural modernity is assimilated into a value system guided by religious criteria. In so doing, Islam is repudiating a condition of supremacy by an alien culture that it perceives as simultaneously corrupt philosophically, exploitative economically, and imperialistic politically.

Islam thereby responds to the sense of frustration not only among the politically awakening Arab masses but also among the even more numerous non-Arabic Moslems of Asia as well as of the growing number of Africans and even black Americans (together soon amounting to more than 1 billion people) who feel themselves denigrated in a world still largely dominated by the richer, white, and quasi-Christian West. The Islamic world is deeply aware of the massive attack on its values and traditions, especially in America, which happens to be the spearhead of the modernist revolution and where anti-Moslem expressions often assume crude forms. Islam's current success as a proselytizing faith is in part derived from such resentments, but it is due even more to its offer of a comprehensive vision of an alternative way of life.

Thus in different ways, the spreading concern in the richer countries with ecology (the new faith of the prosperous) and of the great religions with social injustice conspire to help elevate the problem of inequality into the central issue of our times. But while religions can intensify the worldwide concern with the issue of inequality, it is far from clear whether they can provide a concrete model as the answer to the felt need for an effective and globally appealing social order. Christianity can perhaps stir the West's conscience and Islam can mobilize Moslem resentments. But neither at this stage offers a practical response to the central dilemma. There is neither a viable Christian economic model nor an Islamic example of a modern society. At the same time, the failure of communism as an economic system has placed in disrepute any utopian attempt at the implementation of coercive egalitarianism.

In effect, the current and growing concern with the issue of equality is characterized by ideological confusion that is inimical to the sudden emergence of comprehensive dogmas of utopian social reconstruction. The field is dominated more by inchoate longings that find greater emotional satisfaction in ethnicity and even irrationality, to which quasi-fascism could become most responsive. That could lead to a spasm of new political irrationality, even if no longer to the appearance of new and comprehensive metamyths. In that context, the preoccupation with global inequality is likely to express itself through political receptivity to the appeal of a concrete model and a specific leader that

appear effective in defying the richer West and in shaping a
social order that is stable and capable of coping internally with
massive social injustice.

None of the currently developing countries is likely to qualify
as such a model and a leader. India itself manifests the extremes
of wealth and poverty, and thus—even assuming that its ethnic
and religious diversity does not prompt its disintegration—it is
not likely to regain the international stature that it once com-
manded in the days of Nehru. None of the African nations has
the prestige and none of the Latin American ones the vocation
to do so.

Under certain circumstances, as noted earlier, Russia may
be tempted to seek that leadership. Geopolitical dilemmas and
ideological confusion may drive it that way. But Russian leadership, to be accepted by others and not just claimed by the Russians, would have to be based on a working and attractive
socioeconomic model. A quasi-Fascist Russia would be incapable of generating one, with its probable and inevitably debilitating
embroilment in new imperial struggles. A successfully democra-
tizing Russia would be oriented toward the West and would
also be dependent on its continued support; thus its progressive
integration with the advanced world would preclude a close and
ideologically significant identification with the peoples of the
former Third World. Hence if a Fascist or even a democratic
Russia were to pursue such farfetched ambitions, it would still
be unlikely to receive a congenial reception from the world's
deprived.

In contrast, China may have that mantle of leadership thrust
upon itself. China, just by being itself, defies the world of inequality. It is a giant, embracing more than 1 billion people
engaged in a sustained and, so far at least, successful effort to
struggle against inequality. It is also more than just a nation-
state in a world of nation-states. It is the only state that is at the

same time a genuinely distinct civilization. It is certainly much more so than Russia. It thus stands in a somewhat unique relationship to the rest of the world, part of it and yet apart from it.

Over the centuries, that isolation was in large degree self-imposed. It was in part an expression of cultural self-sufficiency and of cultural superiority. China felt that it did not need the world, that in many respects it was above it, and that any attempt at expansion and cultural proselytizing would be pointless. It was also in part defensive, the reaction of a people deeply convinced of their cultural superiority and inclined to defend themselves against barbarian inroads by building walls and closing doors. Even Chinese communism was much less activist on the global scale than its Soviet counterpart, driven by Russian messianism. But that isolation was also a function of distance, geography, and language, all of which (as in the case of Japan) reinforced the self-contained and isolated character of the Chinese civilization.

That self-exclusion is fading. In the modern world, China cannot isolate itself. The world, through mass communications, impacts now on China and China, in turn, increasingly impacts on the world. What happens in China is increasingly visible and important, not only to its immediate neighbors but even to more distant continents. And if China should prove successful in creating, on the scale of more than 1 billion people, a politically viable and, socially, a reasonably adequate society, it will inevitably become, whether it wishes to or not, the focus of significant and growing global interest. For the poorer portions of mankind, starved for a relevant historical guideline, this could be the case even without any Chinese effort to articulate and to propagate ideologically the essence of the Chinese model.

Much, therefore, depends on two broad considerations: what actually happens in China, and how China then chooses to conduct itself on the world scale. Insofar as China's own prospects themselves are concerned, the augury on balance seems favorable. For almost a decade and a half, China has pursued a domestic policy that combined the Marxist veneer with pragmatic economic management, and that combined authoritarian dictatorship with considerable leeway for regional socioeconomic initiative. The result has been the progressive decommunization of the economy, starting with the agriculture (making China, in dramatic contrast to Russia, not only self-sufficient but even into an exporter), expanding to household and retail industries, and the opening up of the coastal regions of China—inhabited by more than 200 million people—to direct participation, through foreign investment and capitalist-style competition, in the wider Asian march toward prosperity. By 1992, the state sector accounted for only about half of the industrial output.

Overall, it has to be said that the Chinese record has been most impressive. Though China remains a poor country by comparative global standards, its GNP has been growing during the 1980s at a rate close to 10 percent per annum. That matches the remarkable pace set earlier by Japan, Korea, and Taiwan. Present indications suggest that China will sustain a similarly high rate of growth during the decade of the 1990s. In some of the coastal regions, such as the province of Guangdong (itself inhabited by more than 60 million people—hence the size of a large European nation), the rate of growth has even reached 13 percent per annum. The assimilation of Hong Kong in 1997 should give further impetus to this growth, especially that of south China. If these rates are sustained, China by the year 2010 could become the fourth global economic power, after the United States, Europe, and Japan.

Moreover, it may reach that state by combining the key elements of the free market system, especially its competitive entrepreneurship (which the Chinese people find quite congenial) and openness to international financial connections, with a residually guiding governmental role, including a still-significant role for state ownership in industry. China's National Information Center estimated in mid-1992 that by 2000, 27 percent of the industrial output (presumably in the main in heavy industry) would still originate from state-owned enterprises, with collectively owned ones contributing 48 percent, and the private sector accounting for the remaining 25 percent. Assuming that improvements in social infrastructure and in personal income were to keep up with the rates of economic growth, China might well come to be perceived by the peoples of many of the developing states, and especially of some of the ex-Soviet republics, as an increasingly attractive alternative to both the failed communist system and the Western-type, free-market-based democracy.

How China chooses to conduct itself on the world scene will therefore be critical. The current octogenarian Chinese leadership will disappear by the mid-1990s by the latest. A period of political instability may then ensue. There is the danger that in such circumstances China might fragment and its economic progress could even be derailed. Chinese history has had a cyclical pattern to it, with periods of effectively centralized power yielding to phases of disunity and fragmentation. This could happen again, especially given the increasingly significant differentiation in the levels of economic development between China's south and north. Were this to happen, China might again turn inward, preoccupied with its internal strife.

However, one has to take into account also the fact that China's socioeconomic advance over the last decade and a half has created the basis for a potentially smoother transition, one that need not be quite as destructive as proved to be the case with Soviet succession problems, which occurred in a setting of evident and intensifying systemic failure. In a more favorable socioeconomic context, the Chinese succession crisis could prove to be less intense and less destructive than normally has been the case with dictatorial systems. In such an event, China before too long might be ready to assume a more assertive global posture.

An economically dynamic and militarily powerful China, increasingly the object of international interest, might then have three grand global options open before it: 1. China, still proclaiming itself to be a communist system even while practicing quite pragmatically what might be called commercial communism, might quite deliberately position itself as the leader of the world's poorer states in opposition to the American-European-Japanese-led coalition defending the status quo; 2. China, translating its economic might into political-military power, might choose to assert its weight in the Asian zone of prosperity, challenging Japanese political preeminence; 3. China, more explicitly abandoning its doctrinal vestiges, might choose to become a member of the global establishment, assuming that it is welcomed into the club.

The first option would doubtless resonate in many parts of the world. To some extent, current Chinese policies seem to be pointed in that direction. China is already providing advanced weaponry to some of the world's most militant developing states, and Chinese rhetoric has been placing increasing emphasis on the unacceptability of a world dominated by the few rich powers. Serious Chinese analyses of world affairs, for example the comprehensive reviews and prognoses contained in the Beijing *Foreign Affairs Journal* of March 23, 1992, have stressed that "The struggle between the developed countries which want to set up a new world order based on Western values and ideologies and the developing countries which oppose such a 'new world order' and propose to set up a fair and reasonable new world order is likely to stand out more sharply."

The temptation to assume a more overt leadership role is likely to grow with the increasing inclination of some leaders of the developing states—and especially of the formerly Communist Russia and Ukraine—to applaud the Chinese model and to encourage the Chinese to articulate more explicitly the conceptual framework of their success. Not surprisingly, this has led the Chinese analysts cited above not only to stress that China will support the just cause of the developing nations but also to assert that "China's international prestige will be largely enhanced by the end of the century." That enhanced prestige (and power) might tempt the Chinese to project an eclectic mixture of Marxism in regard to social issues, quasi-fascism in regard to the role of the state in shaping social priorities, nationalism as the source for political cohesion, and capitalism in regard to economic dynamism.

China could then emerge as the example of an alternative concept of development and as the source of an international challenge to the existing distribution of global power. It is unlikely that its appeal would be in the metamythic style of earlier utopianism but probably it would still have some doctrinal overtones. It would assert that there is a "third way" between the former Soviet communist model and capitalist democracy. In a world increasingly polarized, permeated by weapons of mass destruction, and yearning for a sense of direction that simultaneously expresses outrage and yet serves as a beacon to a better future, China could fill a need that is likely to be in any case widely felt, even in spite of its relative backwardness and linguistic barriers. It could do so both more appealingly and compellingly than Soviet Russia was ever able to do. It could then not only paralyze efforts at international peacekeeping but could contribute quite directly to intensifying warfare in the several Eurasian trouble-spots. Through its economic success, through its arms exports, through its embrace of egalitarian rhetoric, and through its veto in the United Nations, China could aspire to leadership of the global revolt of the masses.

In assessing China's future options, one has to consider also the possibility that an economically successful and politically self-confident China—but one which feels excluded from the global system and which decides to become both the advocate and the leader of the deprived states of the world—may decide to pose not only an articulate doctrinal but also a powerful geopolitical challenge to the dominant trilateral world. The question then arises: what international constellation would best further that goal? For Chinese strategists, confronting the trilateral coalition of America and Europe and Japan, the most effective geopolitical counter might well be to try to fashion a triple alliance of its own, linking China with Iran in the Persian Gulf/ Middle East region and with Russia in the area of the former Soviet Union. Such an antiestablishmentarian coalition could be a potent magnet for other states dissatisfied with the status quo.

Under some circumstances, both Iran and Russia may have good motives of their own to decide to take part in such a Chinese-led triple alliance. Iran might wish to do so in order to secure its traditional imperial ambitions in the Persian Gulf region and in some portions of the formerly Russian Central Asia while also projecting throughout the world of Islam its own special blend of politics and religion. A weakened and frustrated Russia, if its efforts to construct a more democratic and Europe-oriented system should stumble badly, might find association with such a coalition helpful to its own efforts to reestablish at least some portions of the former empire. In both cases, China would have much to offer to its partners—not only weaponry but also the power of a relatively successful socioeconomic system—and each of the partners might, therefore, be prepared to accept for reasons of expediency de facto informal Chinese leadership. To some extent, such a triple alliance would thus resurrect the old Sino-Soviet bloc, but with the formal ideology replaced by a generalized rejection of the inequitable global status quo and with Beijing and Moscow reversing their previous hierarchical relationship.

But even short of assuming such a historically dramatic role, China has a second option. It could pose a serious challenge to regional stability by seeking to assert itself as the principal Far Eastern power. The Far East is already becoming—after the Eurasian oblong of violence—the world's second-most intense concentration of modern weaponry. Every state in the region from Indonesia to Japan is engaged in the process of accumulating advanced weapons. Some, like North Korea and perhaps Taiwan, may soon have nuclear weapons. Thus China's economic power could be channeled in military, rather than ideological, directions. That could eventually pit China against Japan, creating the makings of a major and potentially destabilizing regional rivalry.

The paradox of the region is that it is becoming the world's center in economic activity while lacking any multilateral structure of security. It could thus be prone to the eruption of violence, motivated—in the pragmatic Asian context—not by ideology but by profit. That risk would be heightened by any precipitous U.S. disengagement from the region. Without the U.S. military presence, local conflicts—stimulated in large part by economic interests, such as maritime rights to oil exploration—would then be quite likely to erupt, and China might be inclined to assert itself in that context. Indeed, in some respects the first two options are not mutually exclusive, and some combination of the ideological as well as of the military challenge might be even more likely. In either case, however, the dilemmas of global disorder would become even less susceptible to stable management and the global political process less infused with cooperation.

It follows that China's third option—becoming a member of "the club"—would represent the most desirable future. That, however, will require not only a positive and cooperative Western response—which, in fact, would almost certainly be forthcoming—but also a Western recognition that China will still symbolize, and in part represent, the aspirations of the poorer portions of mankind. China as a world economic power even then will still be, on a per capita basis, a relatively poor, though impressively improving, society. As such, it will in some measure continue to identify itself with the states that are not members of the advanced and richer world. Its example will not only attract others but will tempt the Chinese to articulate the wider meaning of their experience. China will thus still be inclined to act at times as the spokesman, even if not the revolutionary leader, of the global masses.

In any case, the shape of mankind's political future will much depend on the philosophical and cultural evolution of the successful but also rather self-centered West, on the degree to which the postcommunist transformation confirms or refutes the wider relevance of the democratic model, and on the extent to which the world's largest social experiment is, or is not, assimilated into wider global cooperation. In a world of ideological confusion and of social polarization, the specter of geopolitical fragmentation thus clearly threatens. *Global geopolitical dynamics are interacting with the inchoate yearnings of politically awakened mankind for some certainties about its future and for some universally accepted criteria of justice. That agenda is not only daunting; it justifies concern that the dilemmas of global disorder may become the defining determinants of the new age.*

PART V

The Illusion of Control

The twentieth century—the century of metamyths and of mega-deaths—spawned false notions of total control, derived from arrogant assertions of total righteousness. The religious man of premodern times, who accepted reality as God-ordained, gave way to the secular fanatic, increasingly inclined to usurp God in the effort to construct heaven on earth, subordinating not only nature but humanity itself to his own utopian vision.

In the course of the present century, this vision was perverted into the most costly exercise of political hubris in mankind's history: the totalitarian attempt to create coercive utopias. In these utopias, all of reality—on the objective level of social organization and on the subjective level of personal beliefs—was to be subject to doctrinal control emanating from a single political center. The price paid in human lives for this excess is beyond the scope of comprehension.

The manifest failure of that endeavor has given way in the West to the current antithesis, which is essentially that of minimal control over personal and collective desires, sexual appetites, and social conduct. But inherent in the almost total rejection of

203

any control is the notion that all values are subjective and relative. In brief, this century has seen mankind move from experimentation with coercive utopia to the enjoyment of permissive cornucopia, from a passionate embrace of absolutist metamyths to careless toying with relativistic agnosticism.

In that philosophic context, global political conditions are characterized by a dynamic and interactive expansion in:

physical power—over nature, over humanity's life and death, and even over the human being itself through the expanding capacity for scientific self-manipulation;

political activism—with humanity more politically conscious, hence also more susceptible to mass mobilization, and insistent on enhanced participation in decision making;

personal expectations—with both individual and collective ones rising rapidly, especially as the world's rich want more of everything and the poor desire what the rich already have;

pace of societal change—with every generation growing up in a world whose culture, life-style, and social infrastructure tend to be increasingly different from those of its predecessor.

It is an illusion, however, to think that change in any of the above dimensions is truly controlled by mankind. Each is expanding and altering at a pace that is determined by its own momentum. Man does not control or even determine the basic directions of his ever-expanding physical powers. The plunge into space, the acquisition of new weapons, the breakthroughs in medical and other sciences are shaped largely by their internal dynamics. Each innovation breeds another; every expansion of knowledge, skill, or capability is but a step forward, not just in opening ever new doors to the future but actually in leading mankind into that future. The human being, while the inventor, is simultaneously the prisoner of the process of invention.

Much the same is true of the other two major dimensions of our changing reality. Political activism is not necessarily tantamount to the establishment of an effectively functioning democracy. It is, however, a process that involves ever-increasing social demands for participation in decision making, for human rights, and for limits on the unequal distribution not only of power but also of privilege. It transforms a politically passive humanity into an activist mass yearning for a sense of direction.

Personal expectations are being transformed by the accelerating pace with which new products are being introduced—with every new product then generating its own demand—by the consumerist culture of the West that places special emphasis on instant self-gratification, and by the examples that are thereby set for the vast majorities that still mostly watch and envy the life-styles of the fortunate few.

Finally, societal change dramatically alters within the life span of a single generation both the prevailing culture and the socioeconomic infrastructure, and does so at a pace that is at least equivalent to what used to transpire within the time span of a century. The interaction of technology, education, travel, and modern communications has redefined totally the meaning of time and distance and has generated rapid alterations—on the subjective level—in the social mores, and—on the objective level—in the social context.

However, the expansion and the exercise of humanity's powers are not subject to choices influenced by a widely shared moral consensus. In the absence of some shared philosophical criteria that help to define the choices on behalf of which power is exercised, the sheer acquisition and then exercise of power thus becomes haphazard, motivated mostly by self-interest and expediency, and driven by its own inner logic. What appears to be exuberant human liberation consequently becomes dangerous submission to historical forces dominated by the dynamic interaction between technological capabilities and philosophical sophistry.

These broad trends bear very directly on the likely shape of world affairs in the decades to come. A politically activated world, driven by rising social frustrations, even if not soon likely to be infected by a new metamyth, could quite easily become vulnerable to massive instability and violence in the absence of tangible progress, both on the level of political conduct and applied political values, toward an increasingly cooperative and just global system. New spasms of political irrationality would then be likely to manifest themselves.

In such a setting, even though America will remain for some time to come the peerless superpower, its effective global sway may lack authority. American power by itself will be insufficient to impose the American concept of "a new world order." Just as important, the inclination toward cultural hedonism may make it more difficult for America to develop a shared language with those major portions of mankind that will feel they are excluded from meaningful participation in world affairs. As a consequence, they are likely to be on the lookout for some mobilizing message and some relevant example around which to rally in a comprehensive challenge to the global status quo.

In any case, it is almost a certainty that the geopolitical map of the world will become increasingly complex. Instead of a new world order, the states that possesses power and wealth will group together, so that they can better compete against their rivals and so that they can better protect their assets. In specific terms, this foreshadows the emergence of several principal clusters, with America spilling over into some of them but probably with a declining American capacity to decisively determine the internal policies of clusters other than its own. These clusters will be in effect both competitive regional economic blocs as well as political alliances, with the political alliances (especially with America, undertaken for security purposes) in some cases mitigating the economic rivalries.

The probable global power clusters, which will collude, cooperate, and compete with one another within the more interdependent but still unstable global political process, are likely to include:

1. *North America*, dominated by the United States, organized on the basis of the North American Free Trade Area, creating thereby the world's single most powerful economic bloc, and probably also leading in time to the gradual integration of Canada with the United States (perhaps becoming at some point a more formal North American confederation). Its zone of dependence will be the rest of the Western Hemisphere, with Cuba overthrowing its communist system at the latest following Fidel Castro's death.

2. *Europe*, probably integrated economically, but with its political unity lagging considerably behind economic integration, and thus still faced with the problem of a powerful Germany, and with Europe's eastern boundaries in a state of flux, given the continued uncertainties of the postcommunist transition. Its zone of dependence will be both Eastern Europe as well as much of Africa.

3. *East Asia*, dominated economically by Japan, but lacking a commensurate political and security framework, and thus potentially vulnerable to regional tensions, especially as China begins to flex its economic as well as political muscle and perhaps even toys with the notion of assuming the mantle of leadership of the world's deprived. Its zone of dependence is likely to be the far eastern portions of the former Soviet Union, as well as Southeast Asia and also Australia and New Zealand.

4. *South Asia*, likely to lack political and economic cohesion, but at the same time not subject to any massive external political and economic domination, with India as the regional hegemon asserting itself in parts of the region but also opposed by the Islamic states to its west and northwest (including Central Asia).

5. *A shapeless Moslem crescent*, spanning North Africa, the Middle East (except for Israel), perhaps Turkey (especially if it is rebuffed by Europe), the Persian Gulf states and Iraq, and through Iran and Pakistan running northward to embrace the new Central Asian states, all the way to the frontiers of China. It will share in common many of the same aspirations and resentments (especially against the West) but will also be subject to foreign intrusion and will continue to lack any genuine political or economic cohesion.

6. *Perhaps a Eurasian cluster*, a geopolitical "black hole," dominated by a Russia that for some time to come will be struggling to define itself, and covering much of the territory of the former Soviet Union, but overlapping in an imprecise and probably tense manner with three of the above clusters: Europe, Asia, and Islam.

It follows that only the first three clusters will have any degree of political and economic cohesion. The remaining three will be the objects, to varying extents, of some external intrusion and influence, and perhaps also the battleground for rivalries among the first three major clusters. The North American cluster is also likely to be the most cohesive, the only one with a clearly established and unchallenged leader. That will doubtless serve to enhance American power and make it more easy for the United States to play a major role within some of the other clusters.

The American influence will thus continue to be important within Europe, though its scope will be defined largely by the degree to which Europe does or does not move toward deeper and wider integration. While a more united Europe is unlikely to desire complete separation from America, it is almost inevitable that a Europe that acquires a defined political identity will assert itself also vis-à-vis the United States—even if still desiring some continued but much more limited American presence on European soil. A Europe that falters in its efforts to unite, necessarily then more preoccupied with containing Germany's power and perhaps also worried about Russia's longer-range intentions, is more likely to be susceptible to some form of indirect American leadership.

America is also likely to remain influential, though likewise to a declining degree, in the East Asian complex. For one thing, U.S. forces will probably remain for the rest of this decade in both Korea and Japan. That will automatically give the United States an important voice in the region's affairs. For another, the rise of China will introduce major uncertainties, especially in regard to the relationship between the region's two most ambitious powers, China and Japan. The other states in the region clearly desire continued American security involvement, and thus this cluster as well will continue to be influenced by the United States, notwithstanding the region's expanding central role in global economics.

Finally, the United States is almost certain to remain, throughout this decade and into the next century, the central arbiter of the power politics of the Persian Gulf/Middle Eastern region. That will in turn engage America in the internal problematics of the fifth cluster, one that lacks internal cohesion and is most susceptible to foreign intrusion. The long-range danger is that the United States could thereby become embroiled in a protracted engagement in the region's almost endless list of trouble-spots, with the additional risk of a dangerous cultural-philosophical cleavage with the world of Islam, whose theocratic and fundamentalist tendencies the West understandably fears but also tends excessively to denigrate.

The West should understand that the 1 billion Moslems will not be impressed by a West that is perceived as preaching to them the values of consumerism, the merits of amorality, and the blessings of atheism. To many Moslems, the West's (and especially America's) message is repulsive. Moreover, the attempt to portray "fundamentalist" Islam as the new central threat to the West—the alleged successor in that role to communism—is grossly oversimplified. Politically, not all of Islam—in fact, relatively little—is militantly fundamentalist; and there is precious little unity in the political world of Islam. That philosophically much of Islam rejects the Western definition of modernity is another matter, but that is not a sufficient basis for perceiving a politically very diversified Moslem world—which ranges from black West Africa, through Arab North Africa and the Middle East, Iran and Pakistan, Central and South Asia, all the way to Malaysia and Indonesia—as almost ready to embark (armed with nuclear weapons) on a holy war against the West. For America to act on that assumption would be to run the risk of engaging in a self-fulfilling prophecy.

Conflicts between the clusters and within them are also likely. But the former most probably will assume a predominantly economic character. Thus Europe—if it unites and especially if it were to become more protectionist—could become the economic antagonist of the United States, much the way some Americans have come to perceive Japan as America's economic adversary. The Europeans, in addition to their possible collision on global economic matters with the United States, have already become increasingly hostile to Japan's trade practices, and a conflict between the European and the Asian clusters could also ensue. Last but certainly not least, frictions between America and Japan could also intensify, generating a tendency within these two clusters toward a fortresslike mentality, emulating what many expect the Europeans in any case to pursue.

The result would be global economic fragmentation. Protectionism would then flourish, intensified by nationalistic demagogy. While political conflicts, not to speak of military clashes, between the competing clusters would be unlikely to assume grave dimensions, the net result would be quite damaging to global economic growth. The impact on the poorer nations would be especially negative, contributing in turn to intensified political passions and generating an even deeper gap between the rich and the poor.

However, it is somewhat more probable that such an altogether negative scenario will not come to pass. Economic frictions between the major economic powers cannot be entirely avoided. They are an inherent aspect of the competitive and open economic system. Moreover, as national economies cease to be isolated compartments, the emergence of major clusters, which fall short of watertight economic blocs, is almost certain to occur and is actually in the process of occurring. But that need not lead to sharp collisions, and the clusters could become stepping-stones toward a genuinely open world trading system, with the relatively balanced distribution of economic power between the three even encouraging some degree of compromise and accommodation.

Conflicts *within* some of the clusters, however, are likely to be more menacing in their intensity and character. They may, indeed, in some cases even assume quite violent forms. Only the first cluster is likely to be relatively immune to this danger. All of the others are, however, both vulnerable and susceptible to the cumulative contagion of nationalistic passions, economic collisions, and even territorial disputes. It follows that on the level of geopolitics, it is too early to engage in the fashionable dismissal of power politics as a reflection of an age gone by.

Though the Cold War is over, and so are the American-Soviet bipolar struggle for power and its associated East-West ideological collision, some traditional power conflicts are likely to resurface—in addition to the new social and philosophical challenges:

Who controls Europe: an Atlantic coalition involving the United States and a more united Europe; a Europe that is united and stands entirely on its own, with America disengaged; or Germany?

How will the almost inevitable attempt at some—even if only partial—restoration of the Russian Empire evolve and what will its impact be on Central Europe and elsewhere? How will Russia, in any eventuality, relate to Europe (if it becomes more united) or to Germany (if Europe fails to unite)?

How will Japan and China relate to each other, as both gain in power and ambitions, and as the United States disengages from the area?

How will America be able to maintain its position in the Middle East, if its role in Europe and/or the Far East should decline?

In Europe, the decisive question pertains to the pace and depth of Europe's integration. Even with sustained progress, national antipathies will remain strong for some time to come, while some European countries are vulnerable to minority demands for greater autonomy or even for state sovereignty in a larger Europe. But a manifest failure to sustain progress both on the economic and political levels would be likely to reopen some of the geopolitical issues that have been Europe's undoing in the course of this century, in addition also to precipitating new conflicts. The question of Germany's role and orientation would then become again the central preoccupation of European politics. It is to be recalled that Germany has been this century's biggest territorial loser, and in a volatile Europe German resentment of this fact could be suddenly reactivated, with potentially calamitous consequences both for Germany's democracy and for regional stability. That danger could be compounded by socioeconomic failures among the postcommunist countries of Central Europe, not to speak of the temptations of a special relationship between Berlin and Moscow.

In the Far East, the great uncertainty pertains to the future roles both of Japan and China. These two countries are destined to be the region's dominant powers, with Japan inevitably shedding its deference to the United States as it becomes globally more active and with China gradually emerging as a major economic and political actor not just in the region but also on a global scale. A military collision between them is still unlikely but even with the greatest of mutual restraint some tensions and frictions are almost inevitable. At the same time, a number of unresolved territorial issues—particularly those pertaining to the control of maritime exploration rights and perhaps also involving the Chinese-Russian boundary—could generate additional conflicts in the region, involving other countries as well. Profit, rather than ideology or even nationalism, may be the driving motive precipitating unilateral actions in this rapidly developing, increasingly prosperous, but politically unorganized region.

Even more vulnerable to interstate conflicts and internal wars is the South Asian cluster. Parts of it fall into the Eurasian oblong of anticipated violence (discussed in Part IV), but in addition Indian ambitions are likely to produce anxieties among its neighbors. Some, like Nepal and even to some extent Pakistan, rely on China as a source of restraint on India. Some, as for example Sri Lanka, have already been the resentful objects of Indian intervention in their internal conflicts. Finally, India itself may still experience major dissension among its linguistically, ethnically, and religiously diverse population. Attempts at secession are likely, beyond those that have already proven troublesome.

Conflict and instability are likely to remain as central and continuing realities in the Islamic crescent—the arc of crisis—which spans the Middle East and southern Eurasia. Not only are the region's aspiring hegemons in open conflict, with some of them (e.g., Iran) driven not only by religious fanaticism but also by strong imperial traditions, but several of the states in this general area lack any genuine internal cohesion. This is especially the case with the new post-Soviet Central Asian republics. Within them, tribal loyalties are still stronger than a wider sense of national identity. Ethnic violence will, therefore, continue to percolate and periodically explode. Traditional Arab disunity, deliberately abetted by the Western powers interested in retaining control over the Arab supply of oil, will also contribute to persistent regional instability.

Finally, one has to anticipate prolonged tensions as well as occasional outbursts of open violence as the dust settles in post-Soviet Eurasia. It is far from certain that Russia will desist from an attempt to reestablish the old empire. Yet any such attempt will certainly be opposed by some of the non-Russian nations, and this may inhibit open imperialism by the Kremlin. But given the weakness of some of the new non-Russian states, some reconsolidation of Russian influence and even power over them is likely. There may thus emerge some new structure, still euphemistically designated as a "commonwealth," but in which effective political power will again be wielded from Moscow. Some of the agreements concluded in 1992 between Moscow and the governments of the newly "sovereign" republics in effect amounted to the creation of a two-tier Commonwealth of Independent States: some—like Ukraine, Moldova, and Azerbaijan—continue to insist on genuine independence, but others are willing to accept arrangements in economic and military relations that belie their assertions of full sovereignty. That, in turn, is likely to intensify the anxieties of the countries that do want to preserve their newly attained national freedom. In any case, the crisis of Russia's identity is unlikely to be resolved in an entirely peaceful manner.

Accordingly, throughout this decade and into the next century, the world's political affairs will be dominated by issues and conflicts that are the product of conditions, histories, and concerns of an essentially regional character. The world's political power is likely to be distributed in terms of the several clusters discussed above, with some more stable and homogeneous than others, and with America not only dominating one of them directly but still intruding to a significant degree in several of the others. Nonetheless, even American power is not likely to be sufficient to extinguish the fires that are likely to erupt as the political awakening of hitherto dormant peoples escalates into periodic outbursts of regional violence.

In contrast to this political mosaic, the world's ideological discourse in the foreseeable future is likely to be surprisingly uniform, with most governments and with most political actors paying public lip service to the same verities and relying on the same clichés. The failure of the totalitarian challenge, and especially the collapse of the communist model, has meant that almost the entire global dialogue is suffused with ostentatious references and fervent proclamations of fidelity to the democratic ideal. Only very fringe groups dare to profess openly their contempt for or rejection of democracy. Even authoritarian regimes these days tend to define themselves as democracies and espouse democratic sloganeering. This uniformity in expression reflects the waning in doctrinal passions and is mute testimony to the current supremacy—to repeat, on the level of lip service—of the democratic ideal.

It would be a mistake, however, to see the above as a sign of a universal surge in the appeal and staying power of democracy as such. It would be an even more egregious error to confuse the rhetorical uniformity with philosophical consensus. Though the notions of "democracy" are fashionable, in much of the world the practice of democracy is still quite superficial and democratic institutions remain vulnerable. There is no shared global understanding of the real meaning of democracy, and especially to what degree democracy should go beyond the political realm and also entail at least minimum guarantees for individual material well-being. Confusion is even more evident in the case of the concept of "the free market." Today, it is also triumphant—with "Thatcherism" held in higher repute than Marxism. But in many parts of the world the understanding of its inner workings, and of its cultural mainsprings, is quite shallow. Moreover, unless democratic practice, and especially the economic performance of the free market system, leads to a demonstrable improvement in social conditions, it is only a question of time before a negative reaction to these concepts sets in.

The massive failure of totalitarian metamyths, the extraordinary scale of the megadeaths exacted in the name of dogmas, and the currently more pervasive intellectual skepticism regarding the practicality of utopias, makes it unlikely that a self-destructive political wave will replicate the tragic errors of the twentieth century. But a spasm of irrationality, probably reminiscent of the Fascist abomination in style and content—with emotions generated by deep instincts of national identity, ethnic passions, religious beliefs, as well as social and racial resentments, all tapping the hidden wells of mankind's hatreds—could sweep some portions of the globe. Not only are the masses of the poorest countries potentially susceptible; the Fascistic skinheads of Western Europe and their counterparts in other advanced democracies are a reminder that even established democracies nurture their own antibodies. However, the strongest outbursts would most probably take place within those countries that—following the overthrow of totalitarianism—embraced, with naive enthusiasm, the democratic vision and then felt betrayed by it.

It will, therefore, be incumbent on the democratic, more stable, and richer West to promote global conditions that reduce the likelihood of such political regression. This will not be easy, in part because of the West's attitudes toward much of the rest of the world. The West considers itself to be inherently superior, not only on the level of economic development but in political maturity. Much of the West's political rhetoric about the world reflects that attitude: the less developed countries are viewed as politically primitive, economically backward, and religiously fanatic. And while there may be some justification for such feelings, they also tend to betray a patronizing and parochial attitude, insensitive to the historical and cultural factors that prevented other societies from pursuing the same path of development as the West. Moreover, inherent in that attitude is the assumption that historical development is unilinear, and that imitation of the West is the only positive option open to others.

The West's contempt for religion is also part and parcel of this mind-set. Though it focuses most overtly on Islam, it is more generalized. As N. J. Demerath argued in the summer 1991 issue of the journal *Dædalus* dedicated to "Religion and Politics":

> Few conceits have been more enduring in the West than the notion that other societies will inevitably "evolve," "develop," or "modernize." One critical element of this perspective for Western intellectuals involves the secularization motif. Whether defined as the demystification of the sacred, the diminishment of sacred salience, or the sacred's retreat from the societal core,

the process denotes a cultural change that many regard as the inevitable result of such basic developmental processes as Weberian rationalization and Durkheimian differentiation.

Stated more simply, the prevailing orthodoxy among intellectuals in the West is that religion is a waning, irrational, and dysfunctional aberration.

Yet in fact, religion not only persists but in some parts of the developing world is staging a comeback. In addition to the proselytizing efforts of the Catholic church in Africa and Asia, and to the spread also of Islam, evangelical and charismatic Protestantism has been gaining adherents, especially in Latin America and lately in the former Soviet Union. However, the religious revival is often marked by theological confusion and may lack institutional staying power, particularly in the case of the evangelical sects that are dependent on individual and highly charismatic preachers. Nonetheless, it is important to note that the source of the moral sinews of many societies has been established religion, and its heralded decay—especially in the more advanced countries—is not necessarily a sign of human progress.

The absence in the West of any binding moral imperatives perpetuates passivity, if not lack of compassion, regarding the dilemmas of inequality. It is no longer possible for anyone in the West to pretend a lack of awareness of the massive hunger that decimates hundreds of thousands of people each year, and in some years even millions (as recently has been the case in Africa) nor to plead ignorance regarding the appalling poverty and the diseases that characterize the life of large portions of the populations not living either in Western Europe, North America, or the newly prosperous countries of the Far East. Within the much more intimate setting of Europe itself, such selfish indifference has characterized the reaction of the West Europeans to the

painful struggles of their Eastern brothers with the difficult legacies of communism, and much the same could be said about the
attitude of many in America to the plight of America's urban
blacks. Knowledge combined with passivity raises a troubling
moral issue (with a disturbing, though admittedly somewhat remote, parallel to the question that was often put to the Germans
who had lived during the Nazi times), which the West at some
point may find it painful to have to answer.

In the meantime, the gulf in the texture of life—that is to say,
both in its material and in its spiritual dimensions—may widen
between those who increasingly will be able to exploit humanity's
enhanced powers both to gratify and to redefine themselves,
and those for whom life remains dominated by the struggle for
survival in an essentially threatening external world. Immanuel
Kant once defined the end of history as the realization of human
freedom in the context of "a perfectly just civic constitution," at
which point mankind would have fulfilled itself. But what Kant
did not and could not have anticipated was the enhancement of
human capabilities both for material self-gratification and for
increasingly far-reaching scientific self-engineering, thereby re-
focusing man's preoccupation from the externalities of life—
such as the struggle with nature—toward what might be called
the internalities of life—such as gratification of personal desires
(and not just needs) and even capricious self-alteration. The
explosive popularity in the West of cosmetic surgery is a striking,
though superficial, example of the latter phenomenon.

A significant portion of humanity thus finds itself on the
brink of an entirely new era in human affairs. The philosophical
implications of human history being on the edge of a new and
mysterious age are almost mind-boggling. Ultimately, they raise
the question of what is the essence of the human being. But the
more immediate and practical implications are also complex.
They augur a potential dichotomy in global outlook and human

identity that is not only unprecedented but that stands in sharp—indeed, paradoxical—conflict with our age's compression of space and time.

It is ironical that when the world was enormous, separated by weeks and even months of sailing time, the human condition in terms of man's relationship to nature and in terms of man's self-comprehension was in fact much more uniform than it is today, when distance is now only a matter of hours and an instant global perception of events is possible through television. Any further widening of the gulf in the texture of life, though that gulf may be currently somewhat obscured by the universal adoption of democratic rhetoric, will certainly make it more difficult to cope with the world's tangible socioeconomic problems and political dilemmas.

Moreover, it must be recognized that in any case, even under the best of circumstances, progress toward a more genuinely global cooperation—one that begins also to bridge these existential differences—will develop through long stages, will be piecemeal, and at most will be only partial. Slogans about one world, about global justice, or even about a new world order to the contrary, the enhancement of practical cooperation on the global scale, imposing thereby some degree of control over the dynamics of historical change, will be a very slow process, at best minimally ahead of tendencies toward fragmentation and doctrines of irrational escapism. And a positive response will have to manifest itself both on the political as well as the philosophical levels, transforming gradually both the world's distribution of power and its cultural mores.

However, global political dilemmas which are heavily influenced by cultural and philosophical factors cannot be quickly remedied by a few specific prescriptions. Indeed, it must be recognized that the expectation of instant solutions to complex and deeply rooted problems is itself a characteristic of our modern age, with its mind-set heavily conditioned by ideological expectations and technological capabilities. These have induced a reductionist mode of thought, with its inclination to evade sensitive moral and attitudinal problems by imposing on them doctrinal or technical solutions. *The needed correction will not come from a catalog of policy recommendations. It can only emerge as a consequence of a new historical tide that induces a change both in values and in conduct; in effect, out of a prolonged process of cultural self-reexamination and philosophical reevaluation, which over time influences the political outlook both of the West and of the non-Western world. That process can be encouraged by an enlightened dialogue but it cannot be politically imposed.*

In the course of any such process, the West will have to shed its parochial blinders to its own cultural malaise, not only because its spiritual emptiness deprives it of the ability to empathize but also because it would be physically impossible to duplicate on a global scale the West's consumerist society, with its limitless appetite for self-gratification beyond personal need. The non-Western world will have to recognize that the advocacy of con-fiscatory egalitarianism—propounded quite hypocritically by its often corrupt elites—is not the solution, not only because it frightens and alienates the West but also because the recent communist experience demonstrates that as a policy it is a pre-scription for coercive poverty. And all will have to seek a more explicitly defined balance in the modern world between the material and the spiritual dimensions of life, especially if the purpose of global politics is increasingly defined as the progressive shaping of a common global community, with gradually equalizing opportunities for human fulfillment.

In our age the profoundest problems that humanity faces have become too great for the nation-state, the traditional unity of international affairs, to handle. This does not mean that the nation-state has outlived its usefulness or that one should seek to create a world of supranational cartels. The nation-state will remain, for quite some time, the primary focus of civic loyalty, the basic source of historical and cultural diversity, and the prime force for mobilizing the individual's commitment. However, the world today needs more than the nation-state to organize global peace, to promote global welfare, to diffuse globally the fruits of science and technology, and to cope with global environmental problems. All of these things can be done more effectively and rationally if nation-states are encouraged to cooperate in the setting of a larger community that reflects what unites them and submerges what has traditionally divided them.

Accordingly, to institutionalize the progressive emergence of such a common global community new forms of enhanced coop- eration will have to evolve along two major axes: the trilateral relationship among the world's richest and democratic states of Europe, America, and East Asia (notably Japan); and through the United Nations as the wider and more representative frame- work of global politics. This will require a redefinition not only of America's world role but also the adoption by Europe as well as Japan of a broader outlook; and it will require the deliberate enhancement of the UN's political role, even at some cost to the unilateral power of some presently dominant states.

The gradual redistribution of responsibilities within the trilat- eral relationship is needed in order to stimulate a wider apprecia- tion within the more advanced and prosperous portions of the world of a common and shared responsibility both for peace and for peaceful change. As long as that responsibility is wielded, however imperfectly, in the main by the United States alone, both Europe and Japan can feel absolved from having to assume political and moral obligations outside the more immediate areas of their national interest. That self-absolution reinforces their parochialism even as it intensifies American resentments over unequal burden sharing, overstretches American power, and tempts the American public with escapist isolationism.

Thus each of the three will have to alter its predominant mind-set if trilateral cooperation is to be further enhanced. America will have to restrain its missionary impulses and recognize the limits of its power; Japan will have to shed its monopolistic proclivities in world trade and accept limitations on its high-tech ambitions; Europe will have to move beyond its inward preoccupations and be willing to assume larger outside burdens, especially in order to assimilate into Europe some of the former communist states.

As a practical matter, the translation into political reality of the notion of a truly balanced trilateral cooperation will have to mean some devolution of American power to the advantage of Europe and Japan. Some of that devolution has already taken place in financial and economic matters, with the United States compelled to defer more to the views of Japan and Germany in particular. But in time, it should also involve greater European and Japanese participation in political and security decision making, if Europe and Japan are to assume enhanced roles in an increasingly cooperative global political process. There is bound to be some understandable American reluctance to move in that direction. However, without such devolution trilateral cooperation will remain unbalanced, with self-serving European and Japanese parochialism conveniently perpetuated by one-sided American interventionism.

The central purpose of trilateral cooperation should not be just to preserve existing privileges but rather to promote more basic progress in the human condition. That more ambitious goal will also require—in addition to changes in their respective mind-sets—significant changes within each of the three trilateral partners, but especially within America and Europe. America remains, and will remain for some time to come, the world's catalytic nation. Europe is also, though to a lesser extent, especially given the continued worldwide cultural influence of both France and Great Britain. The fact that much of the world looks particularly to America for a preview of its own future imposes a special burden on America to espouse a domestic transformation in its social mores and culture that in turn can provide a meaningful example for others. *The American society cannot be the model for the world—both morally and as a matter of practical economics—if a predominantly cornucopian ethic defines its essence, while a sizable but impoverished minority is simultaneously excluded from meaningful social participation. Preoccupation with the satisfaction of material desires that are growing more and more out of control can only perpetuate and deepen the objective and subjective gulf that is already dividing mankind.*

For Europe to play a more active world role, especially as America's coequal, the decisive precondition is continued unification. Only a more united Europe—the very scale of which defines Europe as a genuine global power—is likely to infuse into the European outlook a more generous global vision. Short of that, Europe will run the risk of reverting to ancient feuds, of remaining selfishly absorbed by its internal problems, and of again becoming preoccupied by its traditional concern with the power of Germany. That is why the promotion of a genuinely united Europe is in the fundamental interest of the world at large. Only such a Europe can undertake, and is likely to be inclined to assume, the larger burdens of participation in the building of a global community.

The renewal of America and the unification of Europe are hence the two basic preconditions for a globally more responsible and historically more effective trilateralism. In that context, Japan will have to follow suit, joining its two occidental partners in a global policy designed to maintain political stability while also promoting social change. Japan—like Europe—suffers from a parochialism that fortifies its selfishness, but—unlike Europe—it is a single national community, and as such its sense of national interest can be more easily reoriented toward wider global concerns both by the example and the pressures emanating from a renewed America and a more united Europe.

Such historically responsive trilateral cooperation can also help to infuse into the United Nations a more constructive sense of direction. *The UN's time has finally come. It is only within the framework of that global organization that the common problems of mankind can be collectively addressed.* In the years to come, the UN will have to be gradually reformed in order to make its structure more consistent with global power realities. As already noted, it is unlikely that in the near future it will prove possible to enlarge the number of states which are permanently represented on the UN's Security Council since any such enlargement would jeopardize the special status of the five powers which enjoy the veto-wielding permanent membership. However, perhaps it might prove possible to arrive at a formula for the enlargement of the council by creating a new category of members with permanent seats but without the right to cast the veto. Such an arrangement might prove more palatable, and thus open the doors for the addition of Japan, Germany, India, Nigeria, and Brazil—thereby also meeting the need for a greater political role in the management of world affairs by some of the key non-Western powers.

The fact that in the course of 1992 the UN was able to mount a major peacekeeping initiative in Cambodia and to provide legitimacy for the humanitarian—though predominantly American—mission in Somalia may justify cautious optimism regarding prospects of UN-sponsored international peacekeeping. But the prolonged failure both of the UN and of the European Community to respond to the bloody crisis in the former Yugoslavia is also a reminder that such international cooperation is still very much constrained by national fears, suspicions, and selfishness. Moreover, one cannot discount the possibility that, before too long, progress toward wider cooperation might be derailed by UN vetoes cast either by a Russian or by a Chinese government that at some point may be tempted by great power ambitions to opt out of the western-led UN consensus.

This is why the enhancement of the role of the UN is likely to be more significant in such less political areas of central concern to human survival as assuring global habitability, environmental lawmaking, a worldwide consensus on population policy, and the encouragement of increased flows of overseas development aid to the poorer states. It is the current cliché to say that these problems represent the new agenda of the world, replacing earlier concerns with the struggle for power. In fact, security threats and power struggles within, and perhaps between, the likely global clusters will persist and will remain a major danger to global stability. The new problems, mentioned above, will not displace the more traditional ones—but will be in addition to them, making the global agenda more complex than ever.

Though efforts to address the new problems are bound to make tangible progress very slowly—given the persisting absence of global consensus—one can still expect that a step-by-step increase in international cooperation will occur. Despite existing global cleavages, an incipient global consciousness of a common destiny, inherent in the growing awareness of the finite nature of resources and the vulnerability of the world's ecosystem, is maturing. That awareness offsets to some degree the tendencies toward the polarization of global outlooks and creates the basis for at least some limited but joint responses, especially in regard to ecological problems.

The UN's growing role is also abetted by the increase in

the number of those who are acquiring a vested interest in a cooperative effort to change the status quo gradually and not violently. The world, in the broadest sense, can be seen as divided into two mankinds, living in two distinct cultures: the rich minority and the poor majority. By the end of the century, the first might number somewhere around 1 billion and the second account for the remaining 5 or so. But the 5 billion are also becoming increasingly differentiated, with perhaps as many as 1 billion of them during the last two decades enjoying a manifest improvement in their material condition as a result of successful economic growth. Their stake in reformist and increasingly cooperative policies is thus likely to grow. That, in and of itself, may not be enough to bridge the deep philosophical and material gulfs dividing mankind—with a resentful majority pitted against a privileged minority—but it might somewhat miti- gate the risk that the UN could become paralyzed by a struggle between hostile coalitions and dominated by a new wave of irrational escapism.

Ultimately, however, the effort to gain control over the collec- tive destiny of mankind will succeed or flounder on the critically important philosophical/cultural dimension. It is this dimension that shapes the critical ideas that guide political conduct. And to the extent that the West is still the spearhead of social progress and of political democratization worldwide, it will need to under- take a difficult philosophical and cultural reorientation. It is crucially important that the West's—and especially America's— crisis of the spirit does not vitiate and undo the West's potential for exercising a constructive influence on world affairs, at a stage when for the first time ever a truly global political process makes feasible a common attempt to shape mankind's future.

To reiterate a point made earlier: cultural and philosophical change is a matter of historical waves and not of disparate policy decisions. That change can be influenced by a heightened moral and ethical awareness but it cannot be directed politically. Change can only come out of a fundamental reevaluation of the core beliefs that guide social conduct and from a recognition of the need for a globally shared concept of the meaning of the good life, with the latter based on notions of self-restraint in social self-gratification. The West's ecological movement— whatever may be said about some of its specific advocacy—may be the first step toward such self-limitation. That may prove to be the movement's greatest philosophical contribution, auguring the emergence of a broader acceptance of the principle of self-denial as the point of departure for a globally shared moral consensus.

Any such consensus has to be derived from the recognition that humanity's control over its destiny requires a moral compass as well as a sense of balance. The exercise of control must be infused with an awareness of the consequences of choice, both in practical and in moral terms, which also implies the need for conscious self-restraint. Being able to alter the environment, or to alter oneself genetically, or to consume more because there is more to consume, or to compound the capacity to inflict mass destruction, is not the exercise of control if the expanding human ability to do so automatically becomes the dominant motive for doing so. *The real alternative to total control is not minimal control or, even worse, the absence of any self-restraint, but public self-control that is derived from some internalized and self-restraining notions as to what is appropriate and what is not.*

The imperative of self-restraint has to apply to all the four major dimensions of change in the character of contemporary world politics. It has to apply to physical power, which has to be deliberately restrained through international agreements and voluntary moral codes, because power now can destroy all of humanity directly as well as indirectly through mindless exploitation of the environment and human self-alteration. It has to apply to political activism, which has to be channeled within defined and respected constitutional frames, lest society become increasingly ungovernable, with the quest for meaningful political participation degenerating into demagogic mobilization. It has to apply to personal expectations, because unlimited self-gratification by the relatively few will not only intensify global inequality for the many but will altogether demoralize both the self-indulgent and the deprived. It has to apply also to societal change, particularly in terms of enhanced educational efforts to inculcate in the public the understanding that long-enduring values need not be abandoned simply because of the onrush of new gadgets and new technologies that alter the external dimensions of social life. In the final analysis, taken together, all of the above mean respect for guidelines inspired by more than expediency.

It is noteworthy that the need for an enhanced moral consciousness is not only advocated by religious authorities but also by more reflective political leaders. Even disillusioned Marxist ideologues are recognizing that life cannot be defined meaningfully only on the basis of material criteria. Note, for example, what Alexander Yakovlev, a former Soviet Politburo member and a close associate of Mikhail Gorbachev, had to say in a major address in 1991 to professors and students at Columbia University about mankind's options:

> Social alternative presupposes choice of the quality of *social development*, and by the same token, the qualities of the human potential being formed through the natural course of new social relations. But what does it mean to speak of *a new quality of society*? A political system? Economic effectiveness? Scientific achievements? Wealth?
>
> No, the new quality of society means elevating man through his morality. (Italics in the original.)

Yakovlev's conclusion was a striking echo of the powerful statement of Pope John Paul II, who in his encyclical "*Centesimus Annus*" proclaimed that:

> Of itself, an economic system does not possess criteria for correctly distinguishing new and higher forms of satisfying human needs from artificial new needs which hinder the formation of a mature personality. . . . It is therefore necessary to create life-styles in which the quest for truth, beauty, goodness and communion with others for the sake of common growth are the factors that determine consumer choices, savings and investments. Even the decision to invest in one place rather than another, in one productive sector rather than another, is always *a moral and cultural choice.* (Italics in the original.)

Moral guidance ultimately has to come from within. The modern age, initiated by the French Revolution, placed a premium on the certainties of the so-called objective truth, spurning subjectivity as irrational. The failure of the most extreme perversion of that mode of political thought—namely, of the totalitarian metamyth—has lately prompted an extreme swing in the pendulum of fashionable postmodern thought: from the intellectuals' fascination with "scientific" Marxism as the epitome of "objective truth" to their currently antithetical embrace of uninhibited relativism. But neither response is likely to provide the framework for a world that has become politically awakened and active. The alternative to total control cannot be amoral confusion out of control.

The global crisis of the spirit has to be overcome if humanity is to assert command over its destiny. The point of departure for such self-assertion must be awareness that social life is both objectively and subjectively too complex to be periodically redesigned according to utopian blueprints. The dogmatic certainties of the modern age must yield to the recognition of the inherent uncertainty of the human condition. In a world of fanatical certitudes, morality could be seen as redundant; but in a world of contingency, moral imperatives then become the central, and even the only, source of reassurance. Recognition both of the complexity and the contingency of the human condition thus underlines the *political* need for shared moral consensus in the increasingly congested and intimate world of the twenty-first century.

Acknowledgments

The ideas expressed in this book were shaped by my work in government, refined by my academic research, and reinforced by observations and travel around the world. In the process, I became increasingly impressed by the elusive yet critical interdependence between public philosophy, political beliefs, and international affairs. This is why this book not only trespasses on all three domains but emphasizes, more than is usually the case with analyses of global change, the interconnection among them. Fortunately, I was able to test my ideas against the critical judgment of my interdisciplinary colleagues at the Center for Strategic and International Studies and also of my colleagues and students at the Paul Nitze School of Advanced International Studies of The Johns Hopkins University, both located in Washington, D.C. To them I owe an important intellectual debt.

My first and most important critic, however, was my wife, Muška. She gave me the confidence to make controversial assertions but she also forced me to rethink some of my categorical postulates. My editor, Robert Stewart, not only improved the clarity of my case but was persuasive in pressing me to define more sharply my main theses. Both truly helped. My agent, Leona Schecter, not only played a critical role in arranging for this book's publication but encouraged me to undertake this effort and made helpful suggestions as to its substance.

Trudy Werner, in charge of my office, was instrumental—as on previous and similar occasions—in keeping my professional life on an even keel, thereby making it possible for me to undertake the sustained effort to write my book while also pursuing a busy schedule of traveling, consulting, speaking, and teaching. Paige Sullivan coordinated as well as directly contributed to the research for portions of this effort, with the helpful assistance of Robert Ahdieh, Johannes Bohnen, Gero Verheyen, Raimo Kaasik, and Barbara Zalewski. They refreshed my historical knowledge through background papers and assembled some of the factual data cited in the book. To all of them, I gratefully acknowledge my obligation.

Index

Abortion, 79
Afghanistan, 163
Age of Reason, 4
AIDS, 106
Ambartsumov, Yevgeniy, 177
American Revolution, 47, 55, 63, 69
Arab states, 162–63, 165
Armenians, 17, 157
Artificial intelligence, 78
Atheism, 68
Atom bomb, 10; *see also* Nuclear
  weapons
Attali, Jacques, 134
Austria, 25
Austro-Hungarian Empire, 3
Azerbaijan, 157

Balkan crisis, 139, 145, 165
Baltic states, 156
Bangladesh, 183
BBC, 49
Beijing Institute for International
  Strategic Studies, 128
Belarus, 139, 156
Belgium, 53
Beria, L., 13
Biological warfare, 164
Biotechnology, 77
Blacks, American, 66, 105, 106,
  190
Bolsheviks, 12, 21, 29
Brazil, 152
Britain, 95, 98, 117, 131, 157, 159;
  in Crimean War, 3; and
  European unification, 136, 137,
  141; and Persian Gulf, 161;
  railroads in, 49; in struggle for
  global preponderance, 91;
  television in, 96
Budget deficit, 109

Bullock, Allan, 30
Buultjens, Ralph, 93

Cambodia, 16
Capitalism: China and, 197;
  inequities of, 58; operational
  culture of, 62; supranational, 92
Catalytic nations, 94, 95, 97, 98,
  100, 117; Japan as, 117–31;
  unified Europe as, 129–46
Catholic church, 61, 132, 188;
  Polish, 169–71
Ceauşescu, Nicolae, 41
Chauvinism, 28, 29, 48, 145;
  French, 142; Japanese, 123
Chemical warfare, 164
China, 18; and Central Asian
  conflicts, 165; civilian war deaths
  in, 8, 9; and collapse of Soviet
  Union, 156, 157, 160; and global
  inequality, 182, 192–200; Japan
  and, 128; mass killings in, 16; as
  nuclear supplier, 165; political
  activism in, 50; and post-
  communist transition, 167; and
  United Nations, 150
Christianity, 131–32, 143, 187–91
Civic consciousness, decline of,
  106–7
Civic freedom, 69
Class conflict, 28; in post-
  communist Russia, 173–74
Coercive utopia, 8, 16–17, 30–44,
  57, 59, 60, 63, 65, 67, 74, 77
Cold War, 145, 149, 150, 156,
  166
Collectivization, forced, 11, 16
Communications, 49–50, 58, 76,
  83, 88
Communist Manifesto, 29

Communists, 18, 36; Chinese, 50;
  doctrines of, 38–43; forced
  resettlement under, 157; mass
  murder of class enemies by,
  11–16; resistance to, 15
Competitiveness Policy Council,
  109, 110
Computers, 78
Concentration camps, Soviet,
  14–15
Congress, U.S., 110
Congress Party (India), 51
Congress of Vienna (1815), 3, 25
Conquest, Robert, 11
Conspicuous consumption, 72
Constitution, U.S., 97; First
  Amendment, 72
Crime, 106
Crimea, 160
Crimean War, 3
Croce, Benedetto, 27
Cuba, 16
Cult of personality, 42, 52
Cultural imperialism, 96
Cultural Revolution, 16
Czechoslovakia, 136, 139

Darwinism, social, 74
Declaration of the Rights of Man,
  27
Deficits, 109
De Gaulle, Charles, 132, 138
Demagogy, 29, 30, 35
Democracy, 75, 183; concept of,
  61; in former communist
  countries, 62, 153, 172, 178;
  international influences on, 93;
  Japanese, 126; morality in, 68;
  political philosophy of, 80
Demoralization, 36–37
Denmark, 143–44
Dogmatism, 28, 29, 59
Domenach, Jean-Marie, 48
Dostoevsky, Feodor, 64
Dresden, firebombing of, 9–10
Drug culture, 106
Dual-use technology, 165

Ecology, 37, 77, 99; and global
  inequality, 185–87
Economic power: American,
  108–11; Chinese, 194–96, 200;
  European, 133–34; Japanese,
  119–27, 129
Education, 104–5, 110; higher, 131
Educational Testing Service, 70
EFTA (European Free Trade
  Area), 136, 139
Egypt, 50, 183
Einstein, Albert, 42
Engels, Friedrich, 41
Entitlements, 99
Estonia, 158
Ethiopia, Italian invasion of, 9
Ethnic violence, 145, 157–59, 165
Europe, unified, 87–88; as catalytic
  state, 129–46; China and, 198;
  and postcommunist transition,
  175–76
Euthanasia, 79

Family, decline of, 106, 113
Famines, 11
Fascism, 29–30, 48, 179–81, 192,
  197
Films, American, 71, 96, 106
France, 24, 98, 117, 131, 132, 161;
  in Crimean War, 3; ethnic
  xenophobia in, 53; and European
  unification, 137–38, 140–42;
  imperialism of, 157; in struggle
  for global preponderance, 19;
  television in, 96
Franco-German Corps, 136, 140
Franco-Prussian War, 3, 28
Freedom: American notion of, 97;
  definition of, 69
Free market, 61–63, 74, 183; postcommunist transition to, 171–73
French Revolution, 21, 23–29, 47,
  55, 57, 59, 63, 69, 81, 88, 94

Genetic engineering, 77, 79–80
Genocide, 10–18, 31
Georgia, 157

Germany, 4, 132, 133; civilian war
    deaths in, 8; ecological concerns
    in, 186; economy of, 87, 111;
    emergence on world scene of, 3;
    ethnic xenophobia in, 53; and
    European unification, 136–38,
    140–44; nationalism in, 24, 28;
    Nazi, *see* Nazis; and post-
    communist Russia, 160; post-
    communist transition in, 168,
    169; poverty in, 130; productivity
    growth in, 110; rearmament of,
    127; in struggle for global
    preponderance, 91; unification of,
    27–28; and United Nations, 152
Gestapo, 30
Glemp, Cardinal, 171
Good life, definition of, 69, 70, 72,
    112
Great Horde, 5
Greece, 165
Greed, 105
Gresham's Law, 70
Gridlock, political, 107, 111
Gulf War, 88, 99–100, 124, 150,
    162
Gypsies, mass killing of, 8, 10

Havel, Vaclav, 61, 81–82
Health care, 104, 110
Hedonism, 113, 143
Herder, Johann Gottfried, 24, 26
Higher education, 131
Hilberg, Raul, 10
Himmler, Heinrich, 30
Hiroshima, 10
Hitler, Adolf, 8, 10, 11, 30–31, 35,
    38–40, 42, 52, 80, 156
Hitlerism, 29, 30, 34, 40, 42
Holocaust, 10–11
Homelessness, 105
Homicide, 106
Hong Kong, 194
Hopelessness, social, 106
Human Genome Project, 79
Hungary, 25, 26; postcommunist,
    136, 139, 168
Hussein, Saddam, 99, 162

Idealism, 23, 26–29, 41, 59
Ideology, 53, 77; communist, 62;
    homogenization of, 92; literacy
    and, 21
Illiteracy, 105
Imperialism, 28, 29, 94–95;
    collapse of, 50; cultural, 96;
    Japanese, 124; Russian, 117, 155,
    163, 174, 177
Indebtedness, American, 104, 109
India, 50, 51, 152, 184, 192; in
    wars with Pakistan, 9, 17, 165
Indonesia, 199
Industrial noncompetitiveness, 104
Industrial revolution, 3, 20, 22–24,
    34, 57–58, 77
Inequality, global, 153, 167,
    182–200; China and, 192–200;
    ecological issues and, 185–87;
    population growth and, 183–84;
    religion and, 185–91
Infrastructure, deteriorating, 105
International Monetary Fund
    (IMF), 99
Investigative journalism, 96
Investment, 104; Japanese, 121, 125
Iran, 156, 159, 162, 163, 198
Iraq, 100; *see also* Gulf War
Iraq-Iran war, 9
Ishihara, Shintaro, 122
Islam, 53, 140, 158, 159, 163, 165,
    187, 189–91, 198
Israel, 162, 163, 165
Italy, 25, 26; Fascist, 9, 29–30

Jacobins, 26
Japan, 18, 109, 193, 194; as
    catalytic state, 117–31, 146–47;
    China and, 198, 199; civilian war
    deaths in, 8; and collapse of
    Soviet Union, 156, 160, 161;
    economy of, 87, 110–11, 119–27,
    129; emergence on world scene
    of, 3; Europe compared with,
    130–34; global prestige of, 89;
    and Gulf War, 100; productivity
    growth in, 110; in struggle for
    global preponderance, 91; and

Japan (*Cont.*)
   total war, 9; and United Nations,
   152
Jews, 39, 40, 163; mass killing of, 8,
   10–11, 13, 18
John Paul II, Pope, 73, 189
Journalism, investigative, 96

Kazakhstan, 158, 160, 164
Kenya, 183–84
Khrushchev, Nikita, 43
Kim Il Sung, 41
Kirghizians, 158
Korea, 127, 156, 160, 194
Korean War, 9
Kosciuszko, Tadeusz, 25
Kossuth, Lajos, 25, 26
Kuomintang, 16, 50
Kurds, 162, 164

Latvia, 158
Lebanon, 164
Lenin, Vladimir I., 8, 11, 16, 21,
   30–31, 35, 41
Leninism, 29, 30, 34
Literacy, spread of, 19–24, 49–52
Lithuania, 15
Litigation, 105
Loytard, Jean-François, 82

Maastricht Summit (1992), 135, 136
Manichaeanism, 21, 28, 31, 48
Mao Zedong, 8, 11, 16, 41, 52
Marx, Karl, 29, 41
Marxism, 29, 64, 68, 169, 175, 188,
   196, 197; failure of, 48
Mass media: adversarial role toward
   government of, 96; social values
   and, 113; transnational, 92; *see
   also* Television
Mass political consciousness, 20;
   class conflict and, 28;
   democratization and, 93; human
   rights and, 96; industrial
   revolution and, 22; literacy and,
   19–22, 50–52; stages of, 52–53;
   urbanization and, 22–23, 51
Maxwell, Robert, 72

Mazzini, Giuseppe, 25
Megadeath, 7–18, 30
Metamyth, 19–32, 34–35, 44, 59
Mexico, 9, 186
Middle Ages, 5
Military power: American, 128, 140,
   166; Chinese, 196, 199;
   European, 130, 132–34, 136,
   140–41; Japanese, 123–24,
   127–28, 130
Miłosz, Czesław, 64–65
Mobutu Sese Seko, 52
Modernity, redefinition of, 81–82
Moldova, 139, 157, 158, 160
Moore, Barrington, Jr., 60–61
More, Thomas, 58, 66
Morita, Akio, 122
Moslems, *see* Islam
Multiculturalism, 96, 107
Mussolini, Benito, 29

Nakasone, Yasuhiro, 122
Napoleon I, 25, 91, 94
National Front (France), 53, 142
Nationalism, 23–30, 59; Chinese,
   197; and European unification,
   142; Japanese, 122–23; Russian,
   159, 179, 181
National Security Council, 97
NATO, 127, 132, 140, 141
Nazis, 9, 10, 13, 18, 31, 35, 36,
   38–42, 57, 156, 180; doctrines
   of, 38–41; former, tried as war
   criminals, 15
Nehru, Jawaharlal, 192
Nielsen Media Services, 70
Nigeria, 152; civil war in, 9
Nkrumah, Kwame, 52
NKVD, 12–15
North American Free Trade Area
   (NAFTA), 129, 186
North Korea, 16, 199
Nozick, Robert, 78
Nuclear weapons, 133, 164–66, 199

Okita, Saburo, 119, 173
Omnibus Trade and
   Competitiveness Act (1988), 110

One-parent families, 106
Organ transplants, 77–78
Orthodox church, 170
Ossetia, 157, 160
Ottoman Empire, 159, 161
Overseas Development Aid, 125

Pakistan, 156, 159, 163; in wars
    with India, 9, 17, 165
Pamphleteering, 20, 21
Panama, 100
Paraguay-Bolivia War, 9
Paris Commune, 21, 28, 29
Permissive cornucopia, xii, xiii,
    64–74
Poland, 15, 24–25; post-
    communist, 136, 139, 168–71, 175
Poles, mass killing of, 8, 10, 11,
    13–14
Population growth, 51, 183–84
Postcommunist transition, 152–53,
    167–81
Postindustrial societies, 52, 58
Poverty, 105, 111, 112; in Europe,
    130; see also Inequality, global
Prisoners of war, 10, 12, 13
Procedural morality, 67–68
Productivity, 104, 110
Propaganda, 21
Progressive taxation, 105
Prussia, 25

Racial/urban problems, 96, 98
Railroads, 49
Rationalism, 23, 27–29, 59
Relativism, moral, 29
Religion, 51, 53; assault on, 27–29;
    and collapse of communism, 61,
    63; erosion of, 64–65, 68–69; in
    Europe, 131–32; and global
    inequality, 185–91; and legal
    system, 67, 68; and natural order,
    33–34
Rio Conference (1992), 99, 186
Roman Empire, 117
Rosenberg, Alfred, 40
Rousseau, Jean-Jacques, 26
Russia: China and, 197–99; in

Crimean War, 3; and European
    unification, 136, 139–40; and
    global inequality, 182, 192, 193;
    imperial, 117, 155, 163, 174,
    177; 1905 revolution in, 29;
    Poland and, 25; postcommunist,
    15, 37, 87, 97, 156–65, 167–81,
    194; and United Nations, 150; see
    also Soviet Union
Russian Union of Industrialists and
    Entrepreneurs, 170
Russo-Japanese War, 3, 117
Rutskoy, Aleksandr, 177–78

Saudi Arabia, 159
Saving, 104; in Japan, 121, 125
Say, Jean-Baptiste, 73
Schlesinger, James, 166
Secondary education, 104–5
Secret Service, 97
Secularism, 28, 34, 41, 59
Servan-Schreiber, Jean-Jacques,
    134
Sexual license, 106
Shiites, 162
Siberia, 160
Sino-Japanese War, 9, 117
Skinheads, German, 53
Slovenia, 139
Social engineering, 77
Solidarity movement, 170
Solzhenitsyn, Aleksandr, 11
Sommer, Theo, 144
Soviet Union, 31, 35, 42–43, 58,
    197; civilian war deaths in, 8, 10;
    collapse of, 89, 136, 149, 152,
    155–65, 175, 176, 183;
    deterrence of military expansion
    of, 61; in global political process,
    98; mass killings in, 11–16; in
    struggle for global preponderance,
    91; succession problems in, 195
Spain, 117
Spanish Civil War, 9
Spirit, crisis of, 54, 107, 173
Spring of Nations, 27
Stalin, Josef, 8, 11–16, 30, 35,
    41–43, 52, 156

Stalinism, 34, 42, 179
Stankevich, Sergei, 177, 178
Strumilin, S., 44
Sukarno, 52
Supreme Soviet Committee for International Affairs, 177

Tadzhiks, 158, 160
Taiwan, 194, 199
Taxation, progressive, 105
Technology: communism and, 59, 62; of death, 10, 17; in developing countries, 76; dual-use, 165; literacy and, 22; of self-alteration, 77
Television, 49–50, 69–72, 96; influence on national values of, 112–13; violence on, 106
Todorov, Tzvetan, 36
Tokyo University, 118
Total war, 9
Totalitarianism, 7–8, 17–18, 29–30, 48, 58, 62; defeat of, 55; idealization of life outside, 59–60; utopianism and, see Coercive utopia
Trade deficit, 104, 109, 121
Training programs, 109–10
Turkey, 156, 159, 165; massacre of Armenians in, 17
Turkmenistan, 160
Twitchell, James B., 112

Ukraine, 15, 139, 156, 158, 160, 164, 165, 178, 197
UNESCO, 50
United Nations, 99, 150–52, 164, 197; Development Program, 184; Security Council, 151, 166
United States: authority of, 102, 164; blacks in, 66, 106, 190; China and, 198; and collapse of Soviet Union, 61, 156, 161, 183; domestic challenges facing, 103–15; ecological concerns in, 186; European challenge to, 130–46; in global political process, 92, 95–101, 149–50;

global prestige and power of, 87–89; Japanese challenge to, 120–29; in nineteenth century, 95; and Persian Gulf, 162–63, 165; "policeman" role for, 166; post–World War II, 117; procedural morality in, 68; Soviet competition with, 43–44; television in, 70–72; in World War II, 117
Universalism, Western, 48, 143
Urban decay, 105
Urbanization, 20, 22–23, 49, 51
Utopianism, 28, 29, 48, 66–67, 88, 197; of communism, see Coercive utopia; failure of, 83; procedural, 73–74
Uzbeks, 158

Vatican II, 189
Vietnam, 16
Vietnam War, 9
Violence, 106; ethnic, 145, 157–59, 165
Volk, 38–39
Volskiy, Arkadiy, 170

Walesa, Lech, 61
Wars, 7–10, 17; civilian deaths in, 8; see also specific wars
Wealthy class, greed of, 105
Weapons of mass destruction, 164–66
Wolfe, Tom, 72
World Bank, 99
World government, 150–51
World War I, 9, 17, 26, 28, 30, 39, 161
World War II, 9, 11–13, 15, 26, 50, 88, 117, 124, 156, 162

Xenophobia, 53, 142

Yeltsin, Boris, 13, 172, 177, 178
Young Hungary Association, 26
Yugoslavia, 10, 15; breakup of, 145, 150, 164

Zhirinovskiy, Vladimir, 178